SOUTHERN RELIGION
IN THE WORLD

GEORGE H. SHRIVER

LECTURE SERIES IN

RELIGION IN

AMERICAN HISTORY

NO. 9

SOUTHERN RELIGION IN THE WORLD

THREE STORIES

Paul Harvey

THE UNIVERSITY OF
GEORGIA PRESS
Athens

© 2019 by the University of Georgia Press
Athens, Georgia 30602
www.ugapress.org
All rights reserved
Set in 11/15 Adobe Caslon by Rebecca A. Norton

Most University of Georgia Press titles are
available from popular e-book vendors.

Printed digitally

Library of Congress Cataloging-in-Publication Data
Names: Harvey, Paul, 1961– author.
Title: Southern religion in the world : three stories / Paul Harvey.
Other titles: George H. Shriver lecture series in
religion in American history ; no. 9.
Description: Athens : The University of Georgia Press, [2019] |
Series: George H. Shriver lecture series in religion in
American history ; no. 9 | Expanded versions of lectures
presented February 27–28, 2018 at Stetson University. |
Includes bibliographical references and index.
Identifiers: LCCN 2019006689| ISBN 9780820355726 (hardback : alk.
paper) | ISBN 9780820355924 (paperback : alk. paper) |
ISBN 9780820355733 (ebook)
Subjects: LCSH: Protestantism—Southern States—Influence. |
Pentecostalism—Southern States—Influence. | Gospel music—
Southern States. | Price, Frank W. (Frank Wilson), 1895–1974—
Influence. | Chiang, Kai-shek, 1887–1975. | Thurman, Howard,
1900–1981—Influence. | Tharpe, Rosetta, 1915–1973—Influence. |
Cash, Johnny—Influence. | Helm, Levon—Influence.
Classification: LCC BR535 .H3855 2019 | DDC 277.5/08—dc23
LC record available at https://lccn.loc.gov/2019006689

For Dale Soden and Jeff Scholes
teachers, colleagues, and friends

CONTENTS

FOREWORD

This volume originated from the 2018 George H. Shriver Lectures in Religion in American History, which were delivered February 27–28, 2018, at Stetson University. This three-part lecture series, presented every other year, was established by George H. Shriver, professor emeritus of history at Georgia Southern University and an alumnus of Stetson University. In creating this lecture series at his alma mater, Dr. Shriver combined two of his academic interests—American history and religious studies. His generous endowment of this series provides funding not only for the lectures but also for a subvention for the publication of the lectures, which have been published since the beginning of the series by the University of Georgia Press. The 2018 lectures were the tenth set of lectures in this series (though this volume constitutes only the ninth published).

After Dr. Paul Croce, professor of history at Stetson University and comember of the Shriver Lectures Committee, and I decided to have the 2018 lectures focus on religion in the American South, I turned for a recommendation for a speaker to Dr. Sam Hill, professor emeritus of history at the University of Florida, a renowned scholar in American religious history and particularly in religion in the American South. Without missing a beat, Dr. Hill told me I should ask Paul Harvey, professor of history and Presidential Teaching Scholar at the University of Colorado–Colorado Springs.

Paul graciously accepted the offer. He later edited and expanded his on-campus lectures, titled "Southern Religion in Global Contexts," into this volume for publication.

The entry into southern religion in Dr. Harvey's lectures was through the life and contributions of four very different persons from the American South: Frank W. Price, a liberal Protestant missionary in China who worked closely with Chiang Kai-Shek and later, in Virginia, was a proponent of racial desegregation; Howard Thurman, who grew up in Daytona Beach, Florida, and went on to become an influential pastor, poet, theologian, and intellectual mentor for the civil rights movement; and Rosetta Tharpe and Johnny Cash, both of whom were musicians who came from Arkansas and whose music was shaped by their Pentecostal backgrounds. (Harvey also included observations on another Arkansas musician, Levon Helm.) Harvey's lectures focused not just on the influence of these figures on the South from which they came but also on their global impact and significance. Harvey clearly demonstrates how these individuals, though different in so many ways, all represent important aspects of the religious life and contributions of the American South.

Now that these lectures are in print, I wish to thank Paul Shriver for his insightful scholarship and gracious spirit; George Shriver for his generous gifts to Stetson University for the creation and endowment of this lecture series; Lisa Guenther, administrative specialist in the Department of Religious Studies at Stetson, for handling many of the details for the lectures and the visit by Paul Shriver; my colleague Paul Croce for his assistance in planning the lectures; and the University of Georgia Press for its publication of this series.

Mitchell G. Reddish, Chair
George H. Shriver Lecture Series
Stetson University

SOUTHERN RELIGION
IN THE WORLD

INTRODUCTION

Religion in the American South emerged as part of a globalized, transnational movement of peoples from the seventeenth through the nineteenth centuries. Ironically, it then came to be seen as the most localized, provincial kind of religion in America, one famously hostile to outside ideas, influences, and agitators. Yet southern religious expressions, particularly in music, have exercised an enormous intellectual influence. Despite its provincialism during the era of evangelical dominance and racial proscriptions, the kinds of expressions coming from the American South have long since gone global.

This book, presented originally as a series of lectures at Stetson University in DeLand, Florida, takes up the theme of southern religion in global contexts. It does so through a set of biographical vignettes that aim to capture different essences of the southern religious experience. I start, somewhat surprisingly, with the liberal Protestant missionary Frank W. Price, whose southern progressive vision for the transformation of China focused on the figure of Chiang Kai-shek, with whom he worked closely during the 1930s and 1940s. Later in his life, following his postrevolutionary exile from China, Price settled in Virginia, authored works such as *Marx Meets Christ*, and led the champions for the desegregation of the southern Presbyterian church. Price's hopes and dreams for a liberal Protestant future at home and abroad had some successes and many failures, but he stands as an excellent representative of how such a vision could survive the tumults of the mid-twentieth century, from the Depression and war to the 1949 revolution in China.

The second chapter features a portion of the life of the native of Florida, black mystic, cosmopolitan, preacher, intellectual, poet, hymnist, and mentor to the civil rights movement, Howard Thurman. He is familiar to scholars, of course, and to Floridians, but his reputation is not at the level of civil rights leaders well known to nearly everyone else: Martin Luther King Jr., Andrew Young, and nowadays even formerly unknown figures such as Pauli Murray.

Howard Thurman (1899–1981) was born during some of the ugliest years of the Jim Crow era and one of the worst possible times to be an African American in the post–Civil War United States. He lived to see the end of Jim Crow, and his career as a teacher, minister, theologian, writer, and mentor helped to bring about its demise. But his career extends beyond being a minister for civil rights, for he was a mystic, a cosmopolitan, a poet, and a seeker. Perhaps most important, his thoughts, ideas, mentorship, and teaching deeply influenced key figures of the civil rights generation, including Pauli Murray, James Farmer, Benjamin Mays, and King. And his role in founding and leading one of the first self-consciously interracial churches in the United States, the Church for the Fellowship of All Peoples, in San Francisco, gave him an institutional space in which to express his vision for the world.

For all he meant to so many people, Howard Thurman is almost unknown to those outside the ken of religious history and civil rights history. Yet his life, and most especially his religious life, is paradigmatic of many important developments and movements in twentieth-century American religion. In particular he combined a cosmopolitan vision, a mystic spirit, and an activist heart for social justice. And he showed a younger generation how those religious impulses could be combined in one person—how the head and the heart could work together in a person's soul and in the world at large.

Thurman himself embodied this quest for internal spiritual enrichment and external engagement with the world. He understood that making the church a social service organization would rob the spiritual energies that made the church what it was in the first place. But he also insisted that disconnecting the church from the world was heresy of a different sort.

Thurman left San Francisco in 1953 and subsequently preached and taught at Boston University until his retirement in 1965. He used his time there to explore the mysticism and cosmopolitanism that he had been pointing to, even as he provided guidance to a generation of students seeking their purpose in life and looking for ways to apply the religion of Jesus both to their own lives and to the problems of the world. Thurman published twenty-one books, including his own autobiography, but his true strength was as a sermonizer. He found his voice through poetry more than prose but in the process articulated a pluralism and cosmopolitanism that came to define the center-left of American Protestantism. He had come from an isolated and provincial part of Florida but became a man of the world. If Benjamin Mays was, in the words of his biographer Randal Jelks, the "schoolmaster of the movement," Thurman was its spiritual mentor.

The final chapter is focused on two figures who taken together represent the face of southern Pentecostalism to the musical world—Rosetta Tharpe and Johnny Cash—with an epilogue devoted to their fellow Arkansan Levon Helm. The great irony to be explored here is that the South developed into the most violent, inequitable, reactionary region in the country but also came to house the soul of the nation's popular culture, especially in the kinds of music—spirituals, gospel, country, and blues—it produced, which would become a foundation for twentieth-century popular song.

Tharpe, Cash, and Helm all came from essentially the same place in the eastern Arkansas Delta, and they served as emissaries of the southern musical tradition to the outside world. By bringing sounds of the religious and secular South to broad national and international audiences, they helped to create the South as a sort of stand-in for the authentic. This is the South that we now think of as Americana—the South whose backbeat, harmonies, and religious enthusiasms provided much of the soundtrack of the world through the second half of the twentieth century.

The end result here is an exploration of southern religion in global contexts. How did a religious culture known for its provincialism and interiority—the kind of religious culture depicted by Wilbur J. Cash and famously parodied by H. L. Mencken—exert such an outsized influence in the world of politics, belief, and culture? The figures explored in the next three chapters give us some answers. I've deliberately selected figures from a wide range of the religious spectrum, from cosmopolitan (Thurman) to mainstream Protestant (Price) to spirit-filled Pentecostalism (via musical ambassadors Cash and Tharpe). In terms of culture, in the long run, Cash and Tharpe have proven to have had the greatest influence. The cosmopolitan and mystic visions of Thurman look increasingly frayed and tattered in the context of the rising white nationalisms and bitter divisions of our era. And certainly Price's dreams came to naught; no one knew that better than Price himself. But the sounds of Cash, Tharpe, Helm, and so many others from the South live on everywhere as a popular culture of the world. As it turned out, the last really became first.

Lost in Translation

Frank Price, Chiang Kai-Shek,
and the Evolution of Protestant Ideas
in East Asia and America

"Things are happening which I cannot write even in my own intimate quiet hour journal," mused the Presbyterian missionary Frank Price in 1941. "God is using me to interpret views back and forth [between the U.S. and Chinese governments]. Government leaders trust me and confide in me. I have opportunities to talk with people of all groups. . . . Keep me true and humble." This journal entry of February 25, 1941, represents the China-born Price's first recorded thoughts on his key role in China's diplomacy during World War II. At this time in 1941, although some aid to China had already been promised, Congress had not yet approved the Lend-Lease program. The prospects for aid were promising, but the money and material were not yet in hand. The Lend-Lease policy could provide hundreds of millions of dollars in aid, technical assistance, and equipment for the war against Japan—today referred to in China as the "Worldwide Anti-Fascist Struggle." Price served as a key part of a group of missionaries and journalists who were pushing the government in that direction. Later that same day in February 1941, Price held a "long conference" with H. H. Kung, a close adviser and relation to Chiang Kai-shek. Price described how he spent much of his time with Kung in "prayer, on our knees, trying to convince [Kung] of [the] seriousness of cleaning up the government." On Tuesday, February 25, three days after this meeting,

Price penned these words in his diary: "I want to be Isaiah. . . .
Keep me true and humble."[1]

During the 1930s and 1940s, Frank Price represented an important liaison between the regime of Chiang Kai-shek and the United
States. He served as something of an ambassador for the Chinese
republican government during the war against Japan and for a few
years in the postwar period. Price was born in China to a southern family originally from Virginia. Price dedicated his life to the
democratization, unification, and progressive Protestant uplift of
China. He worked on behalf of a mainstream liberal Protestantism
in the Middle Kingdom. Price also represented a second generation of missionaries who were active during the second, third, and
fourth decades of the twentieth century. These Protestants moved
away from the evangelicalism of the early missionary heroes and toward a vision of progressive Christianity and Chinese nationalism
and democratization. Ultimately, this vision failed, but not before
it had significant consequences both in China and in the United
States.

And Price's life and significance do not end there. Following his
return to the United States, he became a significant leader of the
southern branch of American Presbyterianism, known as the Presbyterian church in the United States. He authored significant books
that appear all the more remarkable now given his own personal
experience and the Cold War context in which they were written.
Price represents the kind of person discussed in David Hollinger's
recent book *Protestants Abroad*—a missionary whose influence ultimately provided more important in transforming America than in
converting souls abroad.[2]

Like General Joseph W. Stilwell, the American commander in
the China-Burma-India theater during much of the American part
of World War II in Asia, Price gave Chiang disagreeable advice.
Chiang had grown weary of Westerners demanding reform in the
midst of war, and Price invariably did as well. But in the same week
that Chiang demanded Stilwell's recall, Chiang offered Price a pri-

vate home within the official presidential residence in Chongqing. Price managed a Chinese military school during World War II. He upgraded China's War Area Service Corps as a hostel service for American soldiers. Later, he served as the only non-Chinese member of China's United Nations delegation to San Francisco. He also acted as an unofficial marital counselor to Chiang and Madame Kai-shek, baptized Chiang's family, and generated propaganda for the Kuomintang, the Chinese Republican Party headed by Chiang Kai-shek from 1927 until its exile to Taiwan in 1949. Price also translated many of Chiang's wartime speeches and developed a mass education plan for China after World War II.

To Price and his cohort of Protestant progressive liberal internationalists, Chiang Kai-shek spoke almost perfectly the language of Wilsonian idealism and religious progressivism, the very direction that American missions moved in during the first third of the twentieth century. To put it more concisely, Chiang Kai-shek was (for them) an American religious progressive, full of their ideas about the God-ordained movement toward freedom, democracy, and progress. Price personally and frequently advised the Generalissimo, Madame, and the ministers and vice ministers of the Departments of Information and Foreign Affairs and occasionally also the Department of Education. At Chiang's direction, Price also probed at least one provincial government official about his loyalty to the national government. And during much of his relationship with Chiang, from 1930 until 1948, Frank Price (and his brother Harry) served as conduits between the U.S. and Chinese governments. Frank regularly met with Chiang and his staff. Harry enjoyed access to senior officials in the U.S. State Department. Consequently, through Frank and Harry Price, Chiang could communicate directly with the U.S. government, bypassing his own embassy. No other American had such direct lines of communication to Chiang for so long. And no adviser, Chinese or otherwise, could be as candid with Chiang as Frank Price.

Price and Chiang Kai-shek grew up in the same region of China,

and they even spoke the same Chinese dialect. This proved to be
key in Price's relationship with Chiang, as did the shared Christianity of the two. Throughout their relationship, Price remained
loyal, while offering Chiang honest and direct advice. He maintained in his diary, and in conversations with State Department
officials, that he would not support a government whose leaders
were not reform minded. By the time Chiang fled from China in
May 1949, Price had become convinced that Chiang could not lead
China. Price remained in Shanghai as the Communists rolled in.
Frank Price Jr. told one researcher that his father did not go to
Taiwan because, having been a Japanese colony since 1895, Taiwan
was essentially Japanese rather than Chinese, and he wouldn't be at
home there.

Within a month of Price's return to the United States in September 1952, the CIA made an effort to recruit him, which he
quickly rebuffed. He remained a missionary at heart and was too
forthright, honest, and transparent to be a spy. That is the conclusion of the most careful student of Price's life, and it is a conclusion
well supported by the evidence of Price's writings, both private and
public. We don't know, however, what is contained in government
files on Price, which are apparently several thousand pages long, as
the most careful student of his life was unable to get those files de-
classified, despite repeated FOIA requests.[3]

For our purposes here, Price serves as an example of southern religion in global contexts in this sense: he was a primary exponent of
Wilsonian internationalism and progressivism abroad and at home,
minus the racism that afflicted the Wilsonian worldview. His Presbyterianism was that of Wilson's generation and of southern pro-
gressives more generally. We'll start here by surveying his early
years in China and the United States and then examine his relationship with Chiang Kai-shek in the 1930s and 1940s. The chapter
concludes with an epilogue on Price and Chiang Kai-shek in the
years after the Chinese Civil War and discussion of Price's years in

the United States through the years of transformation in the 1950s and 1960s.

Price's vision carried forward the dream of Wilsonian internationalism, thankfully minus the influence of Wilsonian racism. In that sense, Price represented one particular vision of southern religion in a global context. Further, his work in rural China was much like the work of southern home missionaries in reforming American rural life at home. With his roots deep in both southern Presbyterianism (a tradition that always had emphasized the importance of education and uplift) and the liberal Protestant movements of the mid-twentieth century, Price believed he could see a brighter progressive future for Nationalist China. After returning home, he did much the same for southern Presbyterians struggling with their response to the civil rights movement.

Price was a worker more than an intellectual. He was also an activist, hardly ever ceasing in activity, and not at all a mystic. He thus offers a contrast with the figure of Howard Thurman, discussed in the next chapter. And Price, unlike Thurman, remained firmly attached to the Christian tradition. Price thus represents the hopes and aspirations of southern Wilsonian liberal Protestantism as well as its limitations. Frank Price hoped he could be an "Isaiah" for China, a sort of prophet who could speak truth to power but also lead it into a better future. Ultimately, he served as one more American advisor, unable to move history in the direction he wanted. His visions depended on the leadership of Chiang Kaishek, but their interaction, involving one using the other, could not possibly produce the result Price intended. Price's hopes were lost in translation.

Following his years growing up in China with a missionary father, Price was educated at Davidson College in North Carolina (a historic Presbyterian institution) and later at Yale Divinity School, where he drank deeply at the well of Protestant modernists. While

Frank was a Modernist in fact, if not by self-proclamation, he continued to feature Jesus centrally in his theology. In 1920 he gave a speech to the Chinese Students' Christian Association in North America, of which he was the associate secretary, affirming the indispensability of Jesus Christ. Jesus was a "living Personality," he wrote, and his message was one that "reaches deepest into the human heart, touching the springs of action; it reaches broadest into social and world life, making love and the Golden Rule the ideal; it reaches highest to God, calls him Father and bids us pray. It is a religion of hope, of encouragement, of power to change men, of service and sacrifice." Frank's belief in and conception of Jesus was reflected later in the words of Chiang Kai-shek. In his own way, Chiang sounded like a Protestant liberal, not so different from Price—except that Price was the real thing, a Protestant progressive liberal. For a long time he could not see that Chiang was not.[4]

Price himself saw his mission as improving the lives of rural Chinese. As a theological educator in Nanjing and Hangzhou, Price and his colleagues "provided numerous villages with education, medicine, scientific agricultural methods, and better ways to improve health and sanitation. . . . He believed that Christianity was a progressive force for change, and that peace and world order were achievable once the Gospel crossed many boundaries." Price also worked to build an "indigenous Chinese Church free of foreign control and dependency." Price translated Sun Yat-sen's *San Min Chu*, or the "Three Principles of the People," into English and later described Sun as the Chinese version of Patrick Henry, one who "dreamed not simply of a China free from . . . Western exploitation" but also "foresaw democratic and socialistic government for the nation."[5]

"To my mind the first reason we should believe in Jesus is that he was the leader of a national revolution," Chiang Kai-shek said in a radio broadcast in 1938, only about four months after the slaughter in Nanjing in late 1937.[6] American missionaries staked much hope in Chiang Kai-shek, and even more so in his American-educated wife, to lead China to a future that would be both prosperous and Christianized. The story ended differently, but along the way the relationship of Chiang Kai-shek to both Chinese and western Christian traditions invokes many ironies worth exploring.

Chiang Kai-shek's own personal religious and social views consisted of a complex mixture of Chinese (especially Confucian) tradition, liberalism, and belief in science and progress he received from Sun Yat-Sen, together with biblical injunctions and Christian language that got lost in translation, at least partially. Missionaries who promoted and worked closely with Chiang, especially the Presbyterian missionary Price, understood him as a complex figure, but they knew what image needed to be conveyed to western Christian backers and, during World War II, to the American government. Chiang himself knew of the importance of establishing relationships with Protestant missionaries, who could then plead his case with American governmental officials.

To Price and his cohort of Protestant progressive liberal internationalists, Chiang Kai-shek spoke almost perfectly the language of Wilsonian idealism and religious progressivism, the very direction that American missions moved in during the first third of the twentieth century. To put it more concisely, Chiang Kai-shek was (for them) an American religious progressive, full of their ideas about the God-ordained movement toward freedom, democracy, and progress. Or at least they dreamed he could be that.

For a key period from the late 1930s through the late 1940s, Frank Price played a key role in this process. Later suspected (by some on both sides) of being a spy, Price was in reality a propagandist and champion for the war-torn country, who sought to save China from Japanese subjugation and later from authoritarian or Communist rule. His motives were those of a missionary who foresaw a key role for Christianity in uplifting Republican China. His effect on actual policy, though, was minimal. And thus he can be seen as a representative of the difficulty of extending the liberal Christian internationalist dream held by many midcentury missionaries.

During the early twentieth century, Christianity was seen in many parts of East Asia as a liberalizing force, one that went along with other forces in Chinese history moving toward democracy and science. American Protestant liberals began to turn away from older evangelical ideas of missionary work (focusing on the conversion of lost souls), and increasingly they worked to implant progressive ideas of nationalism in places such as China. This culminated in the famous statement *Rethinking Missions: A Laymen's Inquiry after One Hundred Years* (1932), a study from a group of mainstream Protestants that rejected much previous evangelical thinking about the role of missionaries. The Rockefeller-funded commission urged that missionaries move on from older nineteenth-century naïve ideas of a miraculous transformation of individual souls and instead focus their efforts on building national institutions and local churches that could be turned over to Chinese leadership and control. [7]

In the process, a new understanding of Christianity would provide a space for combining forces with other religions to form a more cosmopolitan view. Confucianism, Buddhism, Taoism, and Christianity all had their contributions to make. At the heart of true religion would be a "pure devotion to God's will which is at the same time and inseparably a love for the divine possibilities in other human beings," the end result being a "universal religion," one already reflected in the "piety of the common people of every land." Frank Price focused much of his missionary work on the rural Chinese with whom he identified and devoted much of his academic studies. A transformation of the economics of rural China, he felt, could renew the soul of the country. He eventually latched onto Chiang, believing in Chiang's own self-conception as a savior of the ordinary people of the country.[8]

Married in 1927 into the wealthy Christian Soong family, Chiang's baptism in 1930 came from both Christianity and Confucian filial piety toward his mother-in-law; he had promised her that he would become baptized as part of his marriage in 1927 to Soong Mei-ling. His synthesis of Confucian ethics and political philosophy and Christian doctrine emerged in his New Life Movement in the 1930s. Chiang connected personal and social salvation, particularly after his kidnapping and imprisonment in 1936 and the war events of 1937. Christianity, Bae Kyounghan writes, provided him a path to become a better person "but also for China to be saved and to become a better society." Kyounghan continues, "By late 1938, he had adopted Bible studies and prayer as an integral part of his daily routine, and devout religious cultivation had become part of his life." The older view that Chiang had "adopted" Christianity simply as a political vehicle is not tenable; clearly, Chiang's religious views and practices were genuine, as his diary makes clear. But the view that his genuine religious practices can be seen apart from his political aspirations and his desire to work with missionaries for China's material benefit, expressed in some new scholarship, is also not persuasive. Religious conversion is a complex, culturally constructed experience in any culture and emerges from a variety of emotional, cultural, and pragmatic reasons. Such was the case with Chiang's adoption of Christianity. [9]

Chiang's connection of his personal spiritual destiny with that of China's is remarkable. Frequently in his diary he blames his own sins for China's suffering at the hands of the Japanese: "I only pray that God will soon forgive me for my sins, so that my nation will soon escape from oppression and realize independence," he mused in mid-December 1938. This is the kind of language—of personal piety together with social consciousness—that would appeal to the mainstream Protestant liberals among whom he worked. Thus, it is little wonder they could adopt Chiang as a figure of national salvation as well. "Our entire nation needs faith in revolution, honorable morality and a Christian spirit of sacrifice," Chiang said in 1937.

As he saw it, Confucianism would provide the morality and ethics, and Christianity the spiritual doctrine, of a new China. Particularly after 1938, as his personal practices grew more devout, Chiang came to appear as the sort of Christian that an American missionary could understand, even if those practices remained as a part of his overall program of self-discipline and sacrifice to form a model Chinese citizen and military/political leader.[10]

In his work *Redeemed by Fire*, Xi Lian discusses the dream that Christianity would illumine China's path to modernization and points out that it is an old one. It began with late nineteenth-century reformers and continued through Sun Yat-Sen's revolutions, and then persisted amid the Nationalist regime under what Xi Lian refers to as the "direction of the autocratic Methodist convert" Chiang Kai-shek. Chinese elites such as Chiang, even if "genuine" converts, viewed Christianity as a kind of midwife to give birth to a unified, centralized, prosperous Chinese state. In this sense, they understood Christianity as part of a package (including science, the principles of Sun Yat-Sen, economic development, and the centralization of political sovereignty) to bring the new China to birth, after the century of humiliation. Chiang kept that faith during the long war against Japan, and missionaries such as Price reinforced those views. They, too, retained a Wilsonian idealism, except that, unlike Wilson, they applied it to Asia.[11]

Before the war, as Chiang Kai-shek gradually adopted a more religious rhetoric that combined Confucian and Christian virtues with Sun Yat-Sen's principles, he spoke of a liberal evangelical vision of Jesus as a "leader of a national revolution—a people's revolutionist," as he put it in April 1938. Sun Yat-Sen had written previously that he belonged to "the Christianity of Jesus who was a revolutionary" and attributed the Chinese revolution to the "teachings of the Church." Chiang Kai-shek furthered his mentor's views on the revolutionary nature of Christianity. As Sun Yat-Sen had three principles, so did Jesus, and those were "truth, righteousness, and abundant life." In preaching those, Jesus had aroused his own nation, awakened the "perishing masses so that they would give up the ways of darkness, become new citizens and build the foundations of a new society." Jesus's "revolutionary spirit," he said, "came from His great love for humanity." He concluded, "let us march together towards the Cross, for the regeneration of our nation and for the realization of everlasting peace on earth."[12]

Early in the war against Japanese aggression, Chiang said, "We must not only save ourselves; we must save the world. This is the spirit of Christ—His spirit of self-sacrifice, of love, and of peace. . . . This is the only road that will bring salvation to the state, the nation, mankind, and ourselves." The issue of the war of resistance against Japanese aggression was "one with that of the struggle between the forces of light and darkness throughout the world, a struggle now approaching its climax." The enemy "would plunge the Pacific into the darkness of Hell, while we strive to make it a lighthouse for mankind."[13]

Price translated many of the Generalissimo's documents during the war and advised him as well when certain passages should not be translated (including those in Chiang's book *China's Destiny*, whose Chinese version included a number of broadsides against British and western colonialism that were omitted in the English version). In a sense, the two used each other, each for their own ends. As one scholar puts it, "Price became Chiang's tool in sounding out U.S. public and government opinion, and in trying to influence that opinion on Chiang's behalf," but he adds that "Price's proximity to Chiang did not translate into policies that were either pro–United States or pro-democracy."[14] Price's choices of translations, and Chiang's choice of emphases in his addresses that were meant for a more general or global distribution, indicate their mutual understanding of what rhetoric was needed for their era.

Chiang pitched his wartime addresses perfectly for an American audience. While ostensibly delivered to Chinese soldiers, his rhetoric mirrored American missionary hopes for the personal salvation of Chinese people and the collective salvation of China's national soul. On Christmas Eve 1943, in a speech broadcast on radio to wounded soldiers, Chiang Kai-shek noted the occasion of the birth of Christ and suggested how "his spirit of Sacrifice, and His martyrdom for the truth" could move men's souls. He continued in a passage that mimicked numerous works written by social gospelers, labor organizers, and others through the earlier twentieth century. Jesus, he said, "grew up among an oppressed people at a time when they were suffering bitterly from foreign aggression, and yet for the sake of lofty and eternal ideals He served His own fellow-country and race and poured out his blood freely as a sacrifice for all mankind. That was the secret of His power—such love of others, such fearlessness of death, such noble imperishable character." Or, as he expressed it more succinctly, "we revolutionary soldiers should live and die like Jesus."[15]

The cause, Chiang made clear, was for the Three Principles. The revolutionary soldier sacrificing like Jesus on the cross was fighting for "National Independence, Democracy, and the People's Livelihood—which the Father of our country bequeathed to us and which can save our country and people, mankind and the world." [16]

The following year, as the tides of war grew more favorable, Chiang Kai-shek reflected further on his own interaction with Christianity. He had studied the reasons "animating opposition" to Christianity as well as the essentials of its principles. Eventually, he said, he realized that Jesus was "not only a Savior of mankind but also a leader of national, social, and religious revolution." The principles of Jesus inspired the struggle to bring forth a new world of "freedom, equality, peace, and happiness." Again, just as Christian liberals had argued for decades in America, Chiang Kai-shek suggested that the millennium envisioned by Jesus was not in some ethereal heaven but was meant for the here and now. In the evangelical-speak of America, Chiang sounded like a postmillennialist, one who saw a growing, greater perfection in the world that would prepare the way for the second coming of Jesus.[17]

Missionaries such as Frank Price seized on this language for two reasons. First, it provided the perfect opportunity to present the case to Americans for greater aid to China. Someone who sounded like a modern, progressive Christian, as Chiang did in his addresses, seemed like a worthy recipient of such aid. In addition, though, Price and others used such philosophies to advocate for reform within the Nationalist movement and the wartime government. Other missionaries printed articles on how Chiang and his wife "were engaged in a great crusade to eliminate old evils from Chinese life and replace them with the 'Christian' virtues of cleanliness, patriotism, and self sacrifice."[18]

Price kept up a steady stream of editorials and radio broadcasts early in the war, using his position to advance the cause of the coalition to resist Japanese aggression. Between October 1938 and July 1940 Frank was a prolific propagandist, an editorialist for the biweekly *New China Weekly* newsletters, and a content provider for the China Information Service. Both the *New China Weekly* and the China Information Service served part of a larger effort to provide news for Americans outside the mainstream media. These missionaries, like Price, desperately wanted to see Chiang and China prevail, and they wrote letters accordingly. In Price's case, he contributed vitally to the work of the Department of Information for the KMT, even if he was not employed by the Party proper. He also gave radio broadcasts that attempted to generate support for China. But this does not suggest that Price was simply following orders. Price and others were cooperating with—assisting, rather than working for—the KMT. They were propagandists for the love of China.

Despite knowing that Chiang's government was corrupt, the media were not free, and that unity and democracy in China appeared to be slipping away, Price advanced a message of hope. "Will China maintain her national unity? Will China progress toward democracy?" Price asked. "I have been given absolute freedom to tell you my own impressions and convictions." Price then outlined why Chiang could no longer afford to be patient with the Communists, while also arguing that the Generalissimo intended to maintain freedom of the press. Price outlined improvements in China, specifically mentioning increased agricultural production, industrial development, better education, the fight against opium, better roads, relief programs, and an "unshaken morale," citing all as evidence that China was progressing despite the struggle against both the Japanese and the Communists. Ultimately, he proclaimed that "China is as united as ever in her struggle for freedom." He foresaw that "there will be no civil war in China," for although China's "skies are not yet clear," nevertheless a "brighter day" would come. "Unity and democracy are not disappearing in China, they are growing realities," he said. This was exactly the sort of hopeful rhetoric the Chiangs wanted foreigners to hear.[19]

After February 1941, when Frank Price began a new, clearly defined mission for the KMT, his work with the Chiangs and the KMT focused primarily on regular advice to the president and the president's counselors, particularly in the realm of public diplomacy. In this work he frequently flew between Chengdu, where he lived and worked as a missionary, and Chongqing (the wartime republican capital of China following the fall of Nanjing to the Japanese), where he advised KMT officials. Frank Price advised Chiang, prayed with him, wrote and translated his speeches, gave radio broadcasts, spoke at military academies and youth camps, and acted as an interpreter. But the loudest and most frequent of Price's "quiet" counsel to Chiang was to reform his government. In this, Price was guided by his religious beliefs, and he prayed that God would use him as a messenger for Chiang, as an Isaiah. Thus, his calls for reform were frequent and direct. Price was not a "yes-man," but he loved China and was intensely loyal to its government. He also felt a genuine respect for Chiang. These heartfelt loyalties were not required or even expected from non-Chinese and, despite Frank's constant push for reform, this may explain why both Madame Chiang and the Generalissimo embraced him when so many others around the Chiangs were not trusted.

Price carried out his work in straightforward letters and memos to Chiang. Price worried that the Kuomintang should learn to "save its life by losing it" and that Party affiliation should not be the arbiter of government service: "By a larger vision and greater magnamity, by presenting the opportunity to join a good Party rather than by various forms of force or intimidation, by use of more able men in and out of the Party—the Party would rise in estimation of all the people." The Party should push the second principle of Sun Yat-Sen, "the sovereignty of the people." The government must do more to welcome minority and dissenting views, as this would strengthen the government and "give the people a deeper interest and sense of responsibility. I am much concerned at the indifference to national welfare and lack of unselfish, devoted spirit of public service in many quarters." Price added, "We do need a New Life Movement and a Spiritual Mobilization that will reach the masses of the people," referring thus to Chiang's movement of the 1930s that combined Confucian, authoritarian, and Christian precepts and promoted the "four virtues" (ritual/decorum, rightness/duty, integrity/honesty, and sense of shame/wrongness) through a major national crusade of the KMT, aided and abetted by missionaries (certainly including Price), which resembled both Fascist campaigns in other countries and future slogan-led crusades such as the Cultural Revolution. He reminded Madame Chiang, who often served as a liaison and intermediary for her husband, that he spoke frankly because he loved China, and that he could say things to them that he would not say to Americans, when he emphasized the constructive and positive progress being made (such as in his weekly letters to the China Information Service). And again in April 1941, he urged the continued development of a more "popular base" for the government, with more tolerance for patriotic liberals and more listening to constructive criticism. "Greater freedom for creative thought and action can be given without weakening the authority of the central military command or central government," he reminded Chiang, whose centralizing agenda ran counter to these very sentiments.[20]

Soong Mei-ling Chiang, universally known as Madame Chiang, recognized this. In March 1941, she asked that Price be assigned to work in Chungking, the wartime capital, "so that he could be of service in interpreting China to our friends abroad, and American points of view to us . . . I need not point out to you how very much Dr. Price would be able to help China by presenting a true picture of Chinese affairs to the many foreign visitors who come to Chungking, aided by that fact that Price "would still be connected with your Mission and would be expressing opinions as a private individual, unhampered by any official connection." The response was negative, as the Presbyterian church did not wish to spare him for this service, but two years later Price agreed to be an unpaid advisor to the Generalissimo, after months of urgings by Chiang Kai-shek.[21]

Price carried on an extensive correspondence with "My dear Madame Chiang" during the war, often using the opportunity to provide his advice on how the war might aid in the Reconstruction of China. Just after Pearl Harbor, at that time residing in Chengtu, Price expressed his thoughts on what the war might mean. Like the Generalissimo, he thought that Japan had made a "suicidal gamble" and surely would be beaten (Price even thought it would be within a year). He urged using the war to clear out the "deadwood"; to take action against corruption, "inflation, profiteering, speculation"; and to democratize the process of representative government. He hoped that this would be the time when a few missionaries could try to reopen Christian churches in Communist areas, in part to have a connection with Soviet Russia. Acknowledging that the mission board had vetoed Madame Chiang's request for him to serve in Chungking, Price still desired to give his time and energy "voluntarily aside from my regular mission and institutional duties to China's cause."[22]

Price encouraged Chiang's blending of personal and national salvation, suggesting rites and customs that could be made part of the KMT spiritual calendar. In one undated letter to Chiang, he urged the Generalissimo to extend the work of the Spiritual Mobilization Movement and New Life Movement. He suggested that December 25th could be made a National Revival Day. The combination of Christ's birth and China's rebirth would allow the Party to impart messages from the great Chinese sages of the past along with teachings of the Bible, building a strong moral foundation for the nation. These should be communicated "in a very simple Chinese style, not too long," Price advised. More should be expected from China's educated youth, as they would respond to a "call for high patriotic service and real sacrifice." The plan to require some service from college students had fallen though. Price worried about a swing from an overidealization of China to a disillusionment with its problems and weaknesses. And he pointed out how much the United States had to do to develop this relationship, including elimination of the Chinese Exclusion Act, more military and economic aid, and a firm stance among both America and Great Britain for "freedom and justice in Asia."[23]

Price kept up a steady stream of frank advice to Chiang during the war. He wrote in his diary, "God, help me be an Isaiah to Chiang Kai-shek. So great a man, but with his human limitations of judgement and character." Price often urged a "radical reorganization of the govt. and army under Genl's leadership, and bringing of new and able men into service of the central govt." He reminded Chiang of the "malicious propaganda against the Govt and armies or Genl. Himself," which would "undermine confidence in China," and the need to hear constructive criticism to combat these influences. He urged greater press freedoms and open discussion of problems, adding that "this is the American psychology; when problems can be freely discussed there will be a way out, where discussion is stifled, the tendency is dangerous and must be resisted." He concluded: "Generalissimo, Christian friends throughout the world are praying for you at this time of great crisis. May you be given wisdom, strength and courage to lead China to victory and peace and to full cooperation with our allies. Jesus said, 'He that findeth his life shall lose it; he that loseth his life shall find it.' This is a strange but true statement. I believe that if you and the Kuomintang will lose your life for the sake of all China and a free world you will gain greater life and glory." Chiang responded ten days later, "You have seen and told me many things about China's present conditions and expressed your ideas without reservation. No other true and deep friend has shown such [sincerity], upright-edness, faithfulness and straightforwardness, and finding it in you from this makes me express deeply my respect."[24]

Price had his own version of a postmillennial vision, urg-ing that "we must believe in and strive for what at times seems impossible—a world without racial inequalities, without imperial-ism and aggression, without class conflict, without war. More than all else we shall need the faith that the new world will come not simply by man's efforts but by willingness to obey God and His divine laws of truth and righteousness. The Kingdom comes from heaven into lives, communities, nations that are ready to receive it." With it comes "the divine order, the heavenly society." And as he frequently told Chiang Kai-shek and his wife, assuring them of his loyalties to their cause, "You know how I love China, that it is my adopted home, and that my life is given to China and her people."[25]

Such letters continued through the postwar era, until their rela-tionship effectively ended shortly before the 1949 revolution. "You understand that I talked to you in the way you always want to talk," he wrote in the summer of 1946, "with utmost frankness and ear-nestness. I am a loyal supporter of you and the National Govern-ment but as a Christian friend I must speak the truth and I cannot flatter as many do. The best publicity for China is the publicity given by her friends who understand and love her, who see her greatness and her faults. The best material for publicity is the ef-forts that the government and people of China are sincerely making to improve conditions, to carry out reforms and to bring progress and welfare to all the people. The best answer to the Communist challenge is good, clean government, good officials who love the people, good soldiers who protect the people, good business without speculation and graft, good education which will train for intelligent, helpful citizenship, and wise, good international policies."[26]

Ultimately, Price lost faith in Chiang, and he joined some of his missionary colleagues in comparing Communism to a storm that would blow away years of corruption and inequality and perhaps even clear the way for real reform. He opposed intervention to save the KMT government in China and hoped that eventually, after the Communist revolution, China would find a more moderate path, "but only after years of further struggle and suffering." Until then, he urged that Washington recognize the Communist regime; he had been Chiang's friend but recognized what he saw as the "tragic failure" of Chiang's government.[27]

While Price expressed many sentiments common to Protestant liberals, he would not go as far as did the 1932 report *Rethinking Missions* in terms of melding all religions into one universal expression of human morality. In a letter to the Generalissimo just after the war, in which he praised Chiang's "Christian faith and spirit at this great period in China's history," he suggested that there be a "Christian service of Thanksgiving" at his home. He then reflected on the Roosevelt Memorial Service in Chungking, noting that it was "impressive" but criticizing the "religious element of offering incense and homage to the picture of Roosevelt. This is a Taoist rite and does not seem entirely fitting in a national memorial or celebration. We hope that this feature will not be included in connection with any celebration which your Excellency may preside over in connection with V-J Day. We should honor the memory of Dr. Sun Yat-sen but not begin any superstitious ceremony which might lead to his deification. As a Christian and Christian national leader, we are sure you agree."[28]

The extent to which Chiang got drawn into internal American

religious divisions became clear after the war, when rumors spread of Chiang's conversion to Catholicism. Price doubted the rumors, but had to find out for sure if they were true. The rumors were not without foundation. Chiang considered the Catholic Church more unified, and more reliably anti-Communist, than Protestant liberals, and he had advised the Chinese ambassador to the United States to make connection with Catholic church organizations.[29] Price himself, though a religious liberal, held typical Protestant evangelical views about the antidemocratic nature of Catholicism.

Responding to Price's query, on December 23, 1945, Madame Chiang telegrammed Price that "Generalissimo wishes me to reply that he embraced Christianity not because of political expediency but because of spiritual convictions." The telegram, once publicized through the Religious News Service, had its intended effect, including a denial from the National Catholic Welfare Conference that any such conversion was due. Price felt sure that the Generalissimo would be seen as a Christian, not a sectarian, and would be honored by Catholics even if he was a Protestant. Price reminded Madame Chiang that, while there were many honorable Catholic individuals, "we can recognize all this and yet hold to the faith and experience of the Reformed Churches, the faith of your noble parents and of mine. I believe that Protestantism has been not only a truer form of Biblical Christianity but also . . . a stronger force for freedom and democracy. . . . We certainly do not want religious wars and restriction of religious freedom in China."[30]

Price was part of a Chinese delegation to the United Nations in 1945. He was reluctant, and at first refused. Still, he saw the valuable role he could play: "It would be a great opportunity to help China, to channel liberal ideas to the Chinese delegation, to interpret China to American and the world, to represent the missionary movement . . . to bring Christian ideals to bear on the Conference, to open new doors of service in China, to win new friends, to work in larger setting for Christ in His Kingdom." Finally, he wrote, "I hesitate to accept [this honor], but [it is] also a privilege and opportunity to serve China, my country. God give me the wisdom and courage to continue my service to China and Gimmo in most fruitful way. May I be a prophet to China's leaders and to China. Have decided after long thought and prayer to go to S.F." In response to the Generalissimo's invitation to become his personal adviser, Price replied five days later, on April 3, that "I am greatly honored to be appointed as your personal consultant. But I am extremely ashamed since my talent and knowledge are too poor for this position. Being so honored by the Chairman, however, how can I be ungrateful and refuse?" Price was the only non-Chinese member of the Chinese delegation.[31]

Late in the 1940s and even after the Communist revolution, like others, Price believed Christianity might modulate the practices of the Chinese Communist Party. He hoped that Christianity would "leaven the new dough" and bring out a "truly democratic rural society in China." "Surely there are points of contact to be found between the Christian church and this tremendous revolutionary movement," he mused. He believed there to be a "reservoir of goodwill" for Americans in China, and one could not hurry a softening of the Communist attitude. Americans, he concluded, should care about the underprivileged classes in China, not the elites, saying, "we should favor a socialistic approach to China's problems."[32]

Remarkably, given the Cold War context of the 1950s, many other Protestant mainline missionaries maintained some hope that Christianity could flourish even in Red China; they opposed McCarthyite simplicities about a bipolar world divided between freedom and slavery. However, Price's long-held faith in Chiang as the carrier of China's destiny proved to be flawed. As well as he knew China, he could not quite put Chiang Kai-shek in the context of Chinese thought and culture. He saw Chiang as a Protestant convert, which was true. But Price never quite grasped the emphasis on authoritarianism and democratic centralism in Chiang's thought. This is doubly ironic since Chiang followed Sun Yat-Sen's model in this regard. "The Christian world," Price wrote in 1948, "should rejoice that China in her crisis has had such a leader, and pray that he may be given wisdom, grace, and strength to guide his nation aright through years of building."[33]

On Sunday, December 24, 1950, after a lifetime of mission work in China, Frank preached there for the last time; it was his final official public act as a China missionary. Ever trying to reach the people, while using language acceptable to the new political regime, he preached a sermon titled "The People's Christ," in which he hailed the coming of "the century of the common man," depicting the Bible as the "people's book" and Jesus as a "man of the people."[34] Ultimately, however, Communism rather than Christianity sparked the revolution, dashing the hopes of Frank Price's generation. Price himself lived under house arrest from 1950 to 1952 before being released and returning to the United States to serve in leadership positions in the southern Presbyterian church.

Conservative anti-Communists in the late 1940s adopted Chiang as one of their own, understanding him to be an advocate for the same ideas they themselves held. It helped that Chiang grew more visibly pious as he aged and had become fluent enough in Christian thought to help in translations of the Bible. Price became the object of an intense denunciation movement just after the 1949 revolution, which focused particularly on his close relation to the American governmental presence as well as his long relationship with Chiang. Price wondered about any future for Christianity in a Communist China, making him another target for Chinese Christians in the immediate postrevolutionary era.

Price stood far apart from the Protestant right-wingers, and in his 1957 book *Marx Meets Christ* he presented a thoughtful assessment of what Marxist ideas might teach to Christians, particularly in terms of the effects of social inequality. "It will not do for us to join in the outcry against Communism as all bad, as a frightening demonic force, as our implacable enemy." Marxism would not take such a strong hold if it did not have "some elements of truth and good," he wrote. Marx and Jesus had many parallels. Both started their work at age thirty, were reared in a Jewish home, and expressed the messianic hopes of the people. Marx was attractive as a "intellectual genius and revolutionary symbol," rather than as a personality; Jesus's attraction came from his "noble teaching and saintly life, and supremely of his holy and loving nature." Marx was a political revolutionist, Jesus a spiritual one. But Marxian thought turns violence against class enemies, while "Christian love turns the sword first against evil in oneself."[35]

With words like that, perhaps it's no wonder that, after Chiang moved to Taiwan to establish his government there, Frank Price never met him again, even when he visited Taiwan some years later. The two had served each other's purposes, and in a sense both had failed each other. Lost in translation, their ideas for what each represented—a Protestant Christian nationalist China, on the one hand, and a direct liaison to U.S. government aid on the other— came to naught. Chiang came to represent abroad the movement of American Protestantism at home from liberal postmillennialist internationalism to conservative premillennialist visions of a Cold War Armageddon.

Frank Price was a part of that era, but his views remained firm, well placed in the context of a Protestant liberal internationalism and rural reformism of the 1930s and 1940s. Upon arriving in the United States, where he lived the rest of his life from 1952 to 1974 (ironically dying almost at the same time Chiang Kai-shek did), he served his Presbyterian church, wrote his book *Marx Meets Christ*, and taught at Mary Baldwin College in Virginia. He had lived through, and been a close part of, one of the most extraordinary eras of twentieth-century East Asian history. He was a witness to some of the most important events and movements of twentieth-century China. And his vision had come to naught. Late in his life, suffering from Parkinson's disease and dementia shortly before his death, he experienced hallucinations dating from his last years in China, when he was denounced as an American puppet on the streets of Shanghai by some of his closest former Chinese colleagues. Party officials forced some of them to criticize him publicly as part of Mao's early crusades. Price was a restless, peripatetic person, constantly in motion. His life as a college professor must have been stiflingly boring, although he still took the opportunity to travel around the world when he had the opportunity. Price's vision involved a particular blending of religion and politics that came at the culmination of Protestant triumphalist internationalism, and he lived long enough to see the demise of his version of southern Wilsonian internationalism in Asia.

Conservative anti-Communists in the late 1940s adopted Chiang as one of their own, understanding him to be an advocate for the same ideas they themselves held. His church attendance and frequent prayer sessions in the evening with Madame Chiang were staples of American Protestant depictions. The Daughters of the American Revolution, the American Legion, and institutions such as George Benson's Harding College looked for heroes where they could find them, and they found one in Chiang's struggle against Communism and later in his stand in Taiwan. The textile magnate Alfred Kohlberg, who later claimed (incorrectly) to have formed the "China Lobby," founded the American China Policy Association, a right-wing think tank and activist association that promoted the Nationalists.[36]

Chiang and other major figures and families in the KMT who moved to Taiwan became stalwarts of a more conservative Christianity in China, particularly compared to Chinese Christians who remained on the mainland and looked for an accommodation with the Communists. "They used Chinese Christianity to build their prestige abroad, while certain Protestant leaders used them to build up the prestige and influence of Protestant missions in China," one historian explains. Price became the object of an intense denunciation movement just after the 1949 revolution, focusing particularly on his close relation to the American governmental presence as well as his long relationship with Chiang.[37]

After World War II, the Chinese Civil War, and the removal of the Nationalist government to Taiwan, Chiang Kai-shek grew into a different sort of figure for American Protestants. He became a hero for Protestant conservatives, who saw in him the Christian anti-Communist figure who would lead the charge against the spread of atheistic Communism. They hoped too that Taiwan would became the center for Protestantism, democracy, and progress in Chinese civilization. For them, Chiang was an evangelical, not a progressive. Chiang's authoritarian rule and conversion of churches into symbols for the propagation of KMT propaganda was of little concern (as opposed to the Protestant liberals of an earlier era, who criticized Chiang precisely for these reasons). As they saw it, the devoutly Christian Chiang was all that stood in opposition to atheism and Communism.

The adaptation of Chiang and his religious journey into a journey fitting American narratives continued through the postrevolutionary era. As a bulwark of anti-Communism, Chiang appeared to face down Red China as bravely as Churchill, on his own small island, had stared down the menace of a German-dominated European continent. Chiang appeared now as a conservative Christian leader, spreading the gospel of Jesus, free enterprise, and western democracy on his adopted island. "Taiwan Churches Growing Rapidly," the *New York Times* reported on December 19, 1959, noting that former "savages" on the eastern part of island had adopted Christianity. About one in twenty Taiwanese had converted, the article reported, and some were suggesting that Christianity would become the predominant religion on the island in the future. Billy Graham, the American superevangelist of the twentieth century, traveled there in 1957, holding one of his famous crusades. By his side was Madame Chiang, singing the Methodist hymns that she had grown up with in Georgia. American evangelicals in the 1960s and 1970s frequently heard paeans to Chiang as the beacon of democracy and Christianity in the Far East. Of the actual workings of the KMT government, and of Chiang's continued envisioning of himself as one who blended Confucian ethics with Christian doctrine and Sun Yat-Sen's principles, they heard nothing.

Early in the Taiwan years, the Chiang couple built "Triumph Song Hall," replicating their chapel in Nanking. They went there each Sunday, assuming positions in two large chairs in the front. Their pastor from the postwar years in Nanjing, Chen Weiping, led the rites; Chiang preached on Good Friday. Soldiers had to go listen to the sermons there, sometimes lasting up to three hours, while Madame Chiang held prayer meetings for Chinese Christian women on Wednesdays. In later years, the Chiangs' public piety was always visible, with Madame Chiang responding to Christ's suffering as something she herself had gone through; she felt "not only intellectually but personally attached to God." As before, the Chiangs connected personal piety and national salvation—in this case the salvation of the new nation of Taiwan. Frank Price had no connection to the new nation of Taiwan, and said nothing in public about it in his later years even as he maintained a close interest in mainland China, which was his birthplace and remained his spiritual home.[38]

In the early 1970s, President Richard Nixon dispatched Billy Graham to Taiwan. Preparing his famous "opening" to China, Nixon knew that Chiang was furious. Chiang said that the only American he would meet with would be Billy Graham. Chiang had told Graham that he was a follower of Christ first and Sun Yat-Sen second. As much as Chiang had used the Americans for his purposes, in the end Nixon used the evangelicals who had heroized Chiang to explain to him the new policy of opening up to China. As always, Chiang was as much symbol as substance for American religious leaders, who had for decades enlisted him (unwittingly) in their own internecine debates and made him the main character in a grand drama for which the soul of American Protestantism, and not China, was the central actor. In that sense, Chiang came to represent abroad the movement of American Protestantism at home from liberal postmillennialist internationalism to conservative premillennialist visions of a Cold War Armageddon.

More to the point here, even Americans who knew and understood much about China and were fluent in Chinese language and culture could not help but turn Chiang into a symbol that had as much to do with American religious thought, debate, and aspiration as with Chiang's own views. Chiang Kai-shek thus became a sort of distorting mirror, reflecting more the contentious debates in the United States than the complex congeries of philosophies and leaders competing for Chinese souls through the mid-twentieth century. Chiang himself contributed to this process, with the help of his adept and savvy wife, by articulating his pitches for help in language that spoke to American Christians, including everyone from the Protestant liberals of the 1930s to Billy Graham and the evangelicals in the 1950s and 1960s. Chiang thus served a purpose and function for many sides of the American religious spectrum—from Wilsonian liberals to premillennial conservatives. He was the symbol for an age of a struggle among Protestant liberals and conservatives. And that was precisely because he could serve so many purposes and seem to embody so many ideals, both those imposed upon him and those taken up for his own purposes.

But a final irony arises. The vision of Frank Price for China was basically one that combined Confucian virtues with Christian teachings, American democracy, a revitalized rural life for ordinary farmers, and a European-style, centrally controlled social democracy. That did not happen, either with Chiang or with the Chinese Revolution of 1949. And Price's vision for rural reform came to a horrifying climax in the Great Leap Forward of the late 1950s, which produced perhaps the greatest man-made famine in the history of the world. But in contemporary China, perhaps it is Chiang's vision that is winning after all. For Chiang wanted a centralized, authoritarian state with an autocratic leadership, which would unify China and make it into a great power. That's the vision that is coming to pass—a China with a centralized, dictatorial, unified state that governs over a dynamic economy and draws to its cities masses from the rural countryside that Frank Price had hoped to revive. Frank Price's vision died; the Communist dream of Mao is little more than sloganeering now. But Chiang's vision of a unified, authoritarian, state-capitalist regime, with a strong military exercising regional dominance in its sphere of influence, is the victor. It turns out that his was the vision not lost in translation.

The Meaning of All His Strivings

Howard Thurman's Spiritual Quests

> The goal of life is God! The source of life is God! That out of
> which life comes is that into which life goes. He out of whom
> life comes is He into whom life goes. God is the goal of man's
> life, the end of all his seeking, the meaning of all his strivings.
>
> —Howard Thurman, *For the Inward Journey*

In 2017, I began to consider writing a biography of Howard Thurman, someone who has interested me for a long time. There were parts of his life I didn't know very much about. I began research with a search for other biographies. At that time, none existed. Since then, I learned of a lengthy and definitive forthcoming (to be published in 2020) biography by Peter Eisenstadt, a longtime editor of the Howard Thurman Papers Project. There currently exists a biography of sorts that can be compiled by reading the impeccably scholarly introductions to the five volumes of *The Papers of Howard Washington Thurman*, a project directed for several decades by the scholar Walter Fluker. But that's in a set of scholarly papers that aren't really meant for public consumption; rather, they are meant for scholarly research. In *Visions of a Better World*, Quinton Dixie and Peter Eisenstadt laid out the portions of Thurman's life most directly relevant to his trip to India and meeting with Gandhi in 1935–1936. More recently, one section of Gary Dorrien's *Breaking White Supremacy* provides a beautifully crafted introduction to Thurman's life and thought, set within the context of the long history of the black social gospel movement. But with the exceptions of the forthcoming work by Eisenstadt and two documentary films (*The Psalm of Howard Thurman*, currently in production, and *Backs Against the Wall: The Howard Thurman Story*, which first aired on PBS in February 2019), it is remarkable how little attention the story of Thurman's life has garnered from scholars or from the general public. He hasn't yet made the starting team of African American all-stars of the twentieth century. But he should be on that squad.[1]

Why is Thurman's life and career so little known, at least relatively speaking? (In the next chapter, we will see how a similar fate awaited the life and work of Sister Rosetta Tharpe, at least until recently.) Obviously, Thurman's lack of notoriety may be exaggerated. For example, for those in Florida (and particularly at Stetson University, the site of the lectures that form this book and a place very close to the home where Thurman grew up), he is a recognized figure. The city of Daytona Beach proclaimed one day in 1963 "Howard Thurman Day," honoring its hometown hero with a key to the city and special festivities. But in general, Thurman certainly is not as well known as many others in his field. He's not a household name, and it's easy to see why: he was a mystic, an intellectual, a poet—much more than an activist. He was not on the front lines, or even at the rear, of the civil rights struggle. Thurman didn't appear before the cameras of national television, and he was best known by university students and an intellectual class.

Here, I want to reflect on some major portions of Thurman's life, and in particular to consider what it was that made him so important even though few outside the scholarly world have heard of him or know much about his life. And I want to make his relevance to our contemporary world clear. Given the theme of these lectures, *Southern Religion in the World*, I hope to explore how his version of southern African American religious traditions collided with the global context of a nonviolent movement and how the process shaped and transformed ideas about how to remake the South.

Thurman was foremost a man of ideas, and his ideas formed the basis for remaking not only the American South but also the very texture and contours of religious experience in America. Thurman's background was deeply immersed in the black Baptist tradition. He filtered these traditions through liberal Protestantism, Quaker mysticism, and a universalist cosmopolitanism. In the process, he shaped and transformed ideas about how to remake the American South, the country, and the globe. The full implications of his ideas are still being played out, tested, and explored in various worlds of American religion. Thurman the man is not particularly well known; Thurman's ideas, though, have exercised a deep and wide influence, even among those who have never heard his name. And the basic contradiction of his life, one he fully recognized and appreciated, was how much his poor and provincial background and training within one particular tradition, confined within the walls of the American racial system, gave him the power to speak to diverse audiences looking to find a way out of their own limitations. Thurman the black American from coastal Florida, who struggled his whole life with the demons of American racism, became Thurman the figure of an expansive vision of the potentialities of God within us. He was a spirit who taught people how to unlock their own spirits in their quest for God and in their strivings for human healing and unity.

On September 20, 1958, a mentally disturbed African American woman named Izola Ware Curry came to a bookstore in Harlem in New York City. There, Martin Luther King Jr. was signing copies of his new book *Stride Toward Freedom: The Montgomery Story*. She came to the front of the signing line and took out a sharp-edged letter opener, then stabbed the twenty-nine-year-old minister, who had just vaulted to national prominence through his leadership of the Montgomery bus boycott. King barely survived. Doctors later told him that, if he had sneezed, he could have died. Of course, King later received a fatal gunshot wound in April 1968; Curry lived her days in a mental institution, to the age of ninety-seven.[2]

Resting in the hospital afterward, King received a visit from the African American minister, theologian, and mystic Howard Thurman. The two had met before. Thurman served for years as

Dean of the Chapel at Howard University; then as minister of the Church for the Fellowship of All Peoples in San Francisco during 1944–1953; and then as Dean of Marsh Chapel and Professor in the School of Theology at Boston University during 1953–1965. King was a student there when Thurman first assumed his position in Boston, and he heard the renowned minister deliver some addresses. King later remembered watching a World Series game together in a house with Thurman, but Thurman commented with humorous irony that he was one of the few professors at Boston to have exercised almost no influence on the young King. Indeed, Thurman was far from prophetic about the young King, once recommending another candidate over him for a particular ministerial position.[3] Later, as well, the two were never personally close. Thurman was the age of King's father, and indeed was closely connected with King Senior through his years at Morehouse College in Atlanta. But King was close, intellectually and spiritually, with Thurman. King reportedly carried around his own well-thumbed version of Thurman's best-known book, *Jesus and the Disinherited*, in his pocket during the long struggle of the Montgomery bus boycott.[4]

By that time, Thurman had exercised an outsized intellectual and spiritual influence on an entire generation that became the leadership of the civil rights movement. Thurman's trip to India in 1935–36, where he met Mahatma Gandhi, was a key moment in the translation of the Indian nonviolent struggle for independence to the African American struggle for freedom. No wonder that, at the close of the meeting, Gandhi reportedly told Thurman (according to the account of the meeting published in India) that "it may be through the Negroes that the unadulterated message of nonviolence will be delivered to the world."[5]

Thurman gave the same advice he gave to countless others over the decades: that King should take the unexpected, if tragic, opportunity to step out of life briefly, meditate on his life and its purposes, and only then move forward. By doing so, he could recover in both body and soul. When told how long King had been given to recuperate, Thurman urged him to take an additional two weeks. Thurman wrote:

> When he told me, I urged him to ask them to extend the period by an additional two weeks. This would give him time away from the immediate pressure of the movement to reassess himself in relation to the cause, to rest his body and mind with healing detachment, and to take a long look that only solitary brooding can provide. The movement had become more than an organization; it had become an organism with a life of its own to which he must relate in fresh and extraordinary ways or be swallowed up by it.

King replied to Thurman that "I am following your advice on the question." Thurman noted his approval that "plans are afoot in your own thinking for structuring your life in a way that will deepen its channel," and he hoped that he could discuss with King "the fulfillment of the tasks to which your hands are set."[6]

As Walter Fluker, editor of the Howard Thurman Papers Project, has explained, the private mystic and the public activist found common ground in understanding that spirituality is necessarily linked to social transformation. Private spiritual cultivation could prepare the way for deeper public commitments for social change. King himself, according to one biographer, came to feel that the stabbing and enforced convalescence was "part of God's plan to prepare him for some larger work" in the struggle against southern segregation and American white supremacy. In previous years, some had tagged Thurman as the new Gandhi, the long-awaited messiah for a nonviolent movement in America. Thurman had no such pretensions; he knew he was no such thing. But he served as a mentor for the movement. This role fit his capacity for deep reflection and profound preaching that spread new spiritual understandings. King's stabbing was a bizarre and tragic event, but in some sense it gave him the period of reflection and inner cultivation needed for the chaotic coming days of the civil rights struggle. The prison cell in Birmingham, Alabama, where in mid-1963 King penned his classic "Letter from a Birmingham Jail," also accidentally but critically provided much the same spiritual retreat for reflections that helped transform America.

King quoted and paraphrased Thurman extensively in his sermons during the 1950s and 1960s. Drawing from Thurman, King understood Jesus as an emblem of the dispossessed—both to a group of Jewish followers in ancient Palestine and to African Americans under slavery and segregation. That was precisely why Jesus was so central to African American religious history. Thurman was a private man and an intellectual; he was not an activist, as King was, nor one to take up specific social and political causes to transform a country. But he mentored an entire generation, including King, who did just that. Thurman's lesson to King is that the cultivation of the self feeds and enriches the struggle for social justice. In a larger sense, the discipline of nonviolence required a spiritual commitment and discipline that came, for many, through self-examination, meditation, and prayer. This was the message Thurman transmitted to the larger civil rights movement. Thurman combined, in the words of historian Martin Marty, the "inner life, the life of passion, the life of fire, with the external life, the life of politics."[7]

Beyond the story of King, though, following the life of Thurman introduces us to a long history of religion and the civil rights movement, spanning the 1920s to the 1970s. And beyond that, it gives us a fuller picture of the interactions of twentieth-century black theologies with the worlds of liberal Protestantism, the social gospel, mysticism, interracial projects, and intraracial development in the major educational institutions of the black institutional world. Thurman's active and varied life thus put him in touch with, and gave him influence over, a diverse array of twentieth-century theologies, movements, and philosophies. Born and trained in the South, he left it behind, and yet he returned always to his southern

background and training when reflecting on his life and its significance. He knew how to put his southern life, and religion, in national and global contexts.

THURMAN'S BACKGROUND

Born in 1899 in West Palm Beach, Florida, Thurman lost his father Saul (the man raising him, although apparently not his bio-
logical father) when he was seven years old. He spent a somewhat
lonely childhood in a black neighborhood in Daytona, Florida,
communing more with nature than with other people. His mother
and grandmother were major influences. Thurman grew up in the
Baptist Church, but he was wary of it given that a local Baptist
minister initially had refused to give his father, a proud agnostic
with little interest in churchly pretension and ministerial hypocrisy,
a proper burial. Through hard work and years of struggle and mal-
nourishment, Thurman made his way eventually to a black Baptist high school in Jacksonville, thanks in part to the generosity of
a stranger who met him at a moment when he had no money to
complete the trip and was at a point of complete desperation. For
Thurman, this was one of those coincidences that are not so coin-
cidental; he would not have called it providential, but he saw it as
part of a web of life and connectedness, and later set up the Howard Thurman Educational Trust in part to help others as he had
been assisted on his way. At the high school, he worked himself to
a state of complete exhaustion and became the valedictorian, a pat-
tern of immersion of work followed by physical collapse that would
be his modus operandi for much of his life. Early on in his life, he
staked his success on books and on academic success. His success
there led him to his early affiliations with the Young Men's Christian Association (YMCA), and later to Morehouse College, which
he attended from 1919 to 1923. While at Morehouse, he claimed to
have read every book in its library; later, when he attended a seminary and other institutions with more abundant libraries, he con-

sumed books with the hunger of a near autodidact. His professors
and peers saw him as a man on the rise, and tried to recruit him for
various positions and opportunities, but Thurman was determined
to pursue a theological degree and a ministerial career.

One of Thurman's first major influences was the YMCA, which
gave him some of his first speaking and leadership opportunities.
The YMCA functioned as one of the primary vehicles for carrying
on the social gospel movement in the early twentieth century. It
was a way station for numerous southern liberals and radicals seeking to apply their Christian training to real-world social problems.
The YMCA and Young Women's Christian Association (YWCA) also
sponsored numerous speaking tours, hosted international visits,
and brought together people from widely varying backgrounds and
gave them the opportunity to forge youthful cross-racial alliances.
Thurman later rejected some of the strictures imposed upon him
by the Victorian ethics and conduct required by the YMCA, but it
was an important training ground for his growing immersion in
social gospel ideas. And it afforded him connections with students
and young mentors (including Mordecai Wyatt Johnson, future
president of Howard University) that helped him find the broader
world that he was seeking.

Thurman later attended Morehouse College in Atlanta, a city
he returned to frequently over the next decades. His bitter experiences with the overt racism of the southern city, which was never
"too busy to hate," stayed with him. He was soured by these experiences, but through his training at the historically black Baptist
Morehouse College he met Benjamin Mays (who became a lifelong friend) and others with whom he nurtured decades of cooperation and friendship.

From 1923 to 1926, Thurman received theological training at
the American Baptist Theological Seminary in Rochester, New
York, a place with a rich tradition of modernist and social gospel
ideas. Walter Rauschenbusch had died before Thurman arrived,
but his influence loomed large. Thurman took a special interest in

the classes of Canadian theologian George Cross, who became his primary mentor there. Cross was one of several close white mentors that Thurman had in his younger years. Thurman felt alive in his presence, and Cross, a noted theologian of the era, engaged Thurman in one-on-one talks and sessions where, as Thurman remembered, it, he reduced Thurman's arguments to "ash." But like the others, Cross did not, and really could not, fully appreciate what Thurman had in mind with his training. According to Cross, Thurman should pursue larger things of the spirit, not just restrict himself to the narrow world of the African American struggle. As Thurman remembered it, Cross told him: "You are a very sensitive Negro man, and doubtless feel under great obligation to put all the weight of your mind and spirit at the disposal of the struggle of your people for full citizenship. But let me remind you that all social questions are transitory in nature and it would be a terrible waste for you to limit your creative energy to the solution of the race problem, however insistent its nature. Give yourself to the timeless issues of the human spirit." Thurman appreciated what Cross gave him, but saw that Cross "did not know that a man and his black skin must face the 'timeless issues of the human spirit' together."[8] Cross would not be the last white mentor or colleague of Thurman's to be unable to understand Thurman's commitment both to theological ideas in the abstract and to African American liberation in the flesh.

After receiving theological training in Rochester and serving a church in Oberlin (a black church but one that drew a diverse set of congregants), Thurman spent a semester at Haverford College in 1929, being tutored by the Quaker mystic Rufus Jones, who gave him "confidence in the insight that the religion of the inner life could deal with the empirical evidence of man without retreating from the demands of such experience."[9]

Soon afterward, while living in Atlanta, Thurman's first wife, Katie Kelley, passed away from tuberculosis, sending Thurman into a spiral of depression. Following a trip to Europe and time mourning in his home, Thurman reawakened his friendship of some years with Sue Bailey, who had a black Baptist background in Arkansas similar to Thurman's in Florida. From there, the romance grew, and the couple amplified each other's strengths, with Sue's gregariousness and social skills helping to bring the physically awkward Thurman out of his shell.

In 1932 Thurman accepted a position as Dean of the Chapel and Professor of Religion at Howard University. Under the autocratic but effective leadership of school president Mordecai Wyatt Johnson (with whom a very young Thurman had his first saved correspondence, asking for advice on pursuing a ministerial career), Howard attracted a star assemblage of academic talent and became for a few decades the intellectual nerve center of black America. Benjamin Mays, Thurman's friend from Morehouse and lifelong friend afterward, joined him there, as did the sociologist E. Franklin Frazier, the literary luminary Alain Locke, and the legal education genius Charles Hamilton Houston. Thurman served as a nationally prominent minister and educator at Howard University in the 1930s and 1940s. His sermons drew crowds and gave him some national prominence as a spiritual orator of unique talents. From his post there, he crisscrossed the country on speaking engagements, began some of his first significant writing, and struggled to balance his thoughts on both the potentialities as well as the limitations of Christianity. As well, he investigated the dilemmas of the universal message of Christianity and the particularly distorted expressions of it within the American racial hierarchy.

During the 1920s, Thurman gradually developed his ideas about nonviolence and religion, how nonviolence could be part of the solution to racial problems, and, more broadly, the endemic violence within societies. He became a member of the Fellowship of Reconciliation (FOR) after meeting George "Shorty" Collins, a white man who was the southern field representative for the FOR. Late in the 1920s he wrote an article on pacifism, titled "Peace Tactics and a Racial Minority," in *World Tomorrow*, a leading socialist and pacifist journal.[10] Thurman was not that interested in abstract philosophical ideas of Pacifism with a capital "P." His real motive was opposing violence that people like him faced every day more than challenging militarism in general. The daily violence visited upon African Americans was a symbol of the larger violence afflicting the world. He wanted to walk the streets of Atlanta without fear. And during this time he also developed his ideas about what it meant to hate and the costs of hatred on both sides. For blacks, fighting had dangers because it was possible to "hate people so bitterly that one becomes like them."[11]

Thurman was heavily involved with, but also ambivalent about, the Student Christian Movement (SCM), which he had considered to be too willing to tolerate segregation and mouth pious platitudes. But it was through the SCM that he arrived at the turning point of his life. The main impetus came from the Reverend Augustine Ralla Ram, executive secretary of the Student Christian Movement of India, Burma, and Ceylon. He was a second-generation Christian and committed nationalist, who once had told an audience at Spelman College in Atlanta that "Gandhi's outlook is like that of Christ, many think of him as a second corporate Christ, the living spirit of Christianity." The SCM in India wanted members of a Negro delegation to India to combine a "philosophical, mystical approach of personal religion" with a "practical and ethically compelling demand for social justice."[12]

The turning point of Thurman's life, and the key to much of his later influence, came in 1935–1936. During a six-month period, he traveled with his wife Sue Bailey Thurman as part of the "pilgrimage of friendship" of black Americans to India. At first, Howard Thurman was reluctant to go, and matters were no easier given that the Thurmans had two young children (Olive, the daughter of Thurman's first wife; and Anne Spencer, the daughter of Howard and Sue Bailey Thurman). He did not want to be put in the position of defending indefensible practices in American Christianity and certainly had no desire to be a missionary or proselytizer.

Once persuaded he did not have to do either, he and "Mrs. Thurman" (as he always called her) traveled extensively (together with another black couple from America), spoke to around 140 different audiences, fought off various illnesses and a westernized palate that had trouble accepting Indian-style cuisine, and sought out audiences with prominent Indian thinkers and writers, including Rabindranath Tagore (with whom he did not really connect well, one of the disappointments of the trip) and Mahatma Gandhi, with whom he did.

There were two key moments during Thurman's trip, by his account. While in Ceylon (the present-day Sri Lanka), a lawyer there peppered him with questions concerning the racial hypocrisies of American Christianity and whether other religions (particularly Islam) would better express the aspirations of black Americans. The principal took him aside after an address and asked him what he was doing there. The story took on many versions over the years, but in all the versions Thurman was challenged to defend his being a Christian minister in a land that had enslaved black people; at a time when Christian hymn writers were also slave owners and when one of the very vessels that brought people over was named *Jesus*; and during a period since when "you have lived in a Christian nation in which you are segregated, lynched, and burned," with the occasional lynching even during a church service. The principal concluded, according to the account in *Footprints of a Dream*, "I am a Hindu. I do not understand. Here you are in my country, standing deep within the Christian faith and tradition. I do not wish to seem rude to you, but sir, I think you are a traitor to all the darker peoples of the earth. I am wondering what you, an intelligent man, can say in defense of your position." In other cities, people queried him—"why is the church powerless before the color bar? . . . From a 10,000-mile perspective, this monumental betrayal of the Christian ethic loomed large and forbidding."[13]

Later Thurman traveled along the Khyber Pass. While in Afghanistan, observing trains of camels bringing good along the roadways used by ancient conquerors, he said, "all that we had seen and felt in India seemed to be brought miraculously into focus. We saw clearly what we must do somehow when we returned to America. We knew that we must test whether a religious fellowship could be developed in America that was capable of cutting across all racial barriers, with a carry-over into the common life, a fellowship that would alter the behavior patterns of those involved. It became imperative now to find out if experiences of spiritual unity among people could be more compelling than the experiences which divided them." Thurman's memory of his epiphany later led him to a major experiment in Christian interracialism.[14]

Also during the trip he met with Kshiti Mohan Sen, a scholar of Sanskrit. They spent the morning, as Thurman put it, "sparring for position—you from behind your Hindu breastwork, and I from behind my Christian embattlement." Calling it a "watershed experience of my life," he perceived the two of them having a fusing of religious souls. Thurman saw in Sen what he saw in the Quaker mystic Rufus Jones: the purest form of religion, a simple and direct communication with God. His Hinduism, exemplified in lives of the humble, had a lot in common with Thurman's religion of an outcast, downtrodden, and politically marginalized Jesus. Thurman's Jesus became an honorary Hindu. From that point forward, while Thurman continued calling himself a Christian, increasingly for him Christianity served as more of a starting point than a destination, "as he would wander, increasingly widely, in an interreligious search to realize the unity of God by transcending artificial cultural barriers."[15]

Finally, at the end of the trip in February 1936, the Thurmans and a few others conversed with Gandhi for three hours. Arguably, the conversation changed the course of American race relations from that time forward. When Thurman finally met Gandhi in February 1936, much of the conversation hinged on the meaning of the word "nonviolence," originally *Ahimsa* in Sanskrit. Gandhi explained how the word did not come across fully in English with the negative *non-* at the beginning of the term. In reality, non-violence was a metaphysical force, a truth that underlay the seemingly endless violence of human life. Always given to a love for the mystical, Thurman was fascinated. Sue Thurman, however, pushed back. She challenged Gandhi on how to apply these ideas in a context where black Americans faced lynching. His response was similar to how Gandhi replied later when challenged on whether nonviolence had any relevance for Jews facing Nazi exterminationist policies. Gandhi reached for the concept of self-immolation, meaning a complete removal of one's self from contact with the source of the evil. By some accounts, at the end of the talk, Gandhi mused that "if it comes true it may be through the Negroes that the unadulterated message of non-violence will be delivered to the world." By Thurman's own account, Gandhi ended the meeting by pointing out that the greatest enemy of Jesus in the United States was Christianity itself. Either version plausibly expresses Gandhian sentiment, but the former became the tag line that was published in an account of the meeting published the following year. Both Thurman and Gandhi saw social change coming less from mass movements than "from a handful of persons who had realized the proper techniques for self-mastery and could, by their example, show others the way." Both believed that "without the quest for personal spiritual development, genuine social change becomes impossible." Leaders at the founding meeting of the Southern Christian Leadership Conference two decades later remembered the quotation attributed to Gandhi; they understood themselves to be carrying out Gandhian principles of social struggle.[16]

Coming home from his visit to India, Thurman had new visions for what would be required for racial transformation in American life. After his epic encounter with Gandhi, Thurman kept a heavy teaching and lecturing schedule through the country. At North Carolina College for Negroes in 1942, he told an audience of the gulf between democracy and the American way of life. Blacks, he believed, would be "largely responsible for the soul of America. We are called at this moment of crisis in our nation's history." A reporter who interviewed Thurman in 1942 called him a "mystic with a practical turn of mind," with an understanding of economics, who represented a "Christian likeness of many of the best qualities of Gandhi and Nehru"; he was one of the few men "around whom a great, conscious movement of Negroes could be built," like the Indian one.[17]

Like many on the pacifist left, Thurman was not a proponent of a mass movement of nonviolent civil disobedience. Ironically, in this sense he also heeded the words of Gandhi, who felt that the masses were not yet ready—they were not schooled in the spiritual discipline necessary for such a movement. Instead, Gandhi, and later Thurman, looked to the "small bands of dedicated followers of nonviolent resistance who by the strength of their beliefs would be able to bend great historical forces to their will." If one source of the belief in the power of small-scale transformation came from the apostles and the call of discipleship, another was certainly Gandhi's ashrams. Due to the contributions of Thurman, Mordecai Wyatt Johnson, Benjamin Mays, and others, ideas of pacifism and nonviolence were percolating through the left. This included one Sunday School teacher in Indianola, Mississippi, who told the black scholar Hortense Powdermaker that Gandhi had the right idea and "has Christ in him. . . . It is through love that we will conquer." Few did more than Thurman to advance Gandhi's message. And so the American mantra became: "It may be through the Negroes that the unadulterated message of nonviolence will be delivered to the world." But for Thurman, this would be through small groups of dedicated activists, what he called "apostles of sensitiveness," rather than through a mass national movement. But later, when the latter actually arose, he was delighted by its advent and threw his spiritual resources behind it.[18]

Meanwhile, Thurman was growing restless in his post of Dean of the Chapel at Howard University. In the mid-1940s, he staked his life and future on a risky endeavor: the creation of an experimental interracial congregation in San Francisco. In 1943 the Reverend Albert J. Fisk, a Presbyterian minister and college professor at San Francisco State University, contacted Thurman about finding a part-time divinity student who might be interested in participating in an experiment to form an interracial congregation in San Francisco. He had been put in contact with Thurman by A. J. Muste, a doyen of peace and pacifist groups. At first, Thurman recounted, he did not see a connection between himself and the church, but later, he said, "There was kindling in my mind the *possibility* that this may be *the* opportunity toward which my life had been moving." He felt at home most especially in San Francisco, "with its varied nationalities, its rich intercultural heritages, and its face resolutely fixed toward the Orient." San Francisco was the "ideal center" for his religio-racial experiment. Thurman spoke with Mordecai Wyatt Johnson, the president of Howard, about a leave of absence. Johnson challenged him on how he could possibly support himself, but Thurman replied simply that God would take care of him. Thurman had caught a vision of his own destiny, and it would soon become one of the consuming passions of his life.[19]

Thurman had visited San Francisco for the first time in the 1930s, during a summer when he attended staff meetings of the national YWCA held in Asilomar, California. One summer, he remembered, "when I disembarked from the Oakland ferry and walked down Market Street, I had a sense of coming home that I never felt any place else in the world."[20] Upon moving there in July 1944, it was another cold, foggy summer day he remembered, "but the city loomed before us as the loveliest sight we had ever seen." He felt that he and his wife Sue Bailey Thurman "shared a sudden awareness that destiny rode with us right into the city."[21] For the remainder of his life, no matter where he lived, San Francisco was his home. The poor boy from Waycross, Florida saw in San Francisco the closest approximation he could find to his dream of a universalist cosmopolitanism.

Together with Fisk, Thurman helped to plan what soon came to

THE MEANING OF ALL HIS STRIVINGS

be called the Church for the Fellowship of All Peoples (also known as the Fellowship Church). It was one of the first self-consciously multiracial congregations in American history. There were predecessors from the nineteenth century, including Tremont Temple in Boston, and more recently there had been a variety of interracial religious experiments in Philadelphia, Los Angeles, and other cities. But Thurman had something more permanent in mind.

Thurman moved to San Francisco to pursue what he considered one of the great adventures of his life: to establish an interracial congregation that would defy the conventions by which the great majority of American churches operated. He came during an era of rapid transition. San Francisco was a city of some 630,000 just before World War II; of that population, only about 5,000 were African American. By the end of the war, thanks to a migration westward, approximately 32,000 African Americans lived in the city, and a distinct black neighborhood had developed. Many lived in areas with small rooms and apartments recently vacated by Japanese Americans; about 5,000 Japanese Americans from San Francisco ended up in internment camps. One local National Association for the Advancement of Colored People (NAACP) leader in San Francisco noted that "Caucasian San Francisco turned to the machinery already at hand for the subjugation of the Oriental and applied it to the Negro," referring to residential segregation and unequal treatment in nearly all areas of municipal life.[22]

Just before his arrival, Thurman wrote to Fisk that "we must keep in mind constantly that the kind of church that we are building has never been built in the United States before. We must not hamper the creative form that the spirit of God may inspire, by clinging to the patterns with which we are ordinarily familiar."[23] His work with the Fellowship Church seemed to embody his thoughts in "The Meaning of Commitment," in which he wrote, "Commitment means that it is possible for a man to yield the nerve center of his consent to a purpose or cause, a movement or an ideal, which may be more important to him than whether he lives or dies.

The commitment is a self-conscious act of will by which he affirms his identification with that he is committed to. The character of this commitment is determined by that to which the center or core of his consent is given."[24] He got the itch to "establish empirical validation for what to me is a profound religious and ethnical insight concerning the genius of the church as a religious fellowship"; he wanted to "find out for myself whether or not it is true that experiences of spiritual unity and fellowship are more compelling than the fears and dogmas and prejudices that separate men." And he believed that if every community had such a venture as this congregation, "the Church itself would once again set in motion those spiritual processes which gave to it its original impetus and power."[25]

His vision went back to his days at Rochester Theological Seminary. While at Rochester, he roomed with two white students, something that had never been done before (and technically was against school policy; the Seminary set a quota of two admitted black students per year). Elected as president of his class, Thurman met with the president, who said that Negroes could not really stand being fully accepted by white people and thus he hoped the honor would not go to his head. He was beginning to contemplate the ideas that would eventually find full form in *Jesus and the Disinherited* and in his sermonic addresses. He discovered that segregation worked in both the North and the South, whereas he previously had seen it as a southern problem. He questioned whether the church was simply another secular institution. He asked, "Was it an adjustment that the church had made contrary to its own religious commitment, or was it fundamental to Christian ethnics that racial exclusiveness should be operative?" He eventually answered that the "segregated church as such was a reaction response to the environment, and not inherent in the genius of the Christian faith itself. But nowhere in my experience had I ever seen a Christian church that was a living confirmation of my conviction." As he put it on another occasion, "When I have lost harmony with another, my whole life is thrown out of tune. For the sake of my unity with God, I keep working on my relations with my fellows. This is ever the insistence of all ethical religion."[26]

The Church for the Fellowship of All Peoples had a rocky start. Originally connected with, and heavily subsidized by, the Presbyterian church, Thurman quickly pushed it toward a different vision. The last thing he wanted was a mission church, and even less so a "neighborhood church" when it was clear that racial segregation defined American neighborhoods. If the church remained in the Fillmore district of San Francisco (where it originally was located), he realized, it would quickly become a black church, and nonblack congregants would disappear, defeating the entire purpose of the enterprise. In any event, the church soon outgrew its original location, and it became necessary to move simply for practical reasons of space. He continued resisting being made the object of "charity and condescension" by Presbyterians, however well-meaning they might be, because in that case "the crippling disease that has dogged the vitality and the health of the Christian enterprise would have overtaken us—the deadly disease of condescension. Very quickly we would have become a dumping ground for uplifters and the challenge of the development of an integrated religious fellowship would have bounced off the conscience and hearts of the people. For herein lies the great temptation: *If a man can feel sorry for you, he can very easily absolve himself from dealing with you in any sense as an equal.*"[27]

"As I moved more and more into the center of the process at the church I began feeling the urge to put into written form some of the things that were stirring within me," he later wrote in his account of the church, *Footprints of a Dream*. One of those things stirring was the "weekly meditation written out of the heart of my own spiritual struggle," which appeared in the weekly church calendar. Soon people demanded them for wider distribution, and his written words became a "means for a wider participation in the fundamental idea and an ideal upon which we had set our course."

From there, Thurman's star, and his writing career, were on the rise, as he attracted a national audience for his addresses, soon to be aided by tape recording technology that allowed for his sermons to be captured live and made available to supporters.[28]

Thurman's vision of the church emanated from that. Thurman held a lifelong contempt for the missionary impulse. On the one hand, the will to share with others is honorable and could be seen as a moral imperative. At the same time, it's well-nigh impossible to "hold oneself free from a certain contempt for those whose predicament makes moral appeal for defense and succor." For it was pride and arrogance that had turned the missionary impulse into "an instrument of self-righteousness on the one hand and racial superiority on the other." Christianity calls one to administer to human need, but in the process of doing that, the missionary impulse turned its objects into recipients who were not fully human beings or brothers.[29]

He consistently resisted several models he had seen in the past: the mission church (which invariably became an object of condescension), the social mission or activist institutional church (which could easily lose its spiritual moorings), and the church with no connection to social life (which could easily lose its ethical imperative). His vision was of a church with strong spiritual grounding that would prepare, strengthen, and fill with God's love those who would carry on a struggle for justice in the social world. The church had a social mission, but not one that was direct; it was not the job of the church to organize protests, to become social service agencies, or to directly involve themselves in political life. Rather, as Thurman saw it, individuals in the thick of the struggle should have a place to "be able to find renewal and fresh courage in the spiritual resources of the church. . . . The true genius of the church was revealed by what it symbolized as a beachhead in society in terms of community, and as an inspiration to the solitary individual to put his weight on the side of a society in which no person need be afraid."[30] Thurman's younger years were filled with the fear produced by desperate poverty, lack, racism, and the daily cruelty exercised toward African Americans. His vision was of a world where no one would experience that again.

Half the congregants were black and half consisted of other ethnicities, including a sizable contingent of Asians and white Buddhists who, ironically, proved to be a thorn in Thurman's side, as they envisioned the church as a center for social activism and protest. After an initial period of copastoring with Alfred Fisk, the church became Thurman's own, a kind of trial project for his ideas. The initial commitment spoke of congregants seeking "after a vital interpretation of God as revealed in Jesus of Nazareth whose fellowship with God was the foundation of his fellowship with men," and of people desiring "to have a part in the unfolding of the ideal of Christian fellowship through the union of men and women of varying national, cultural, racial, or creedal heritage in church communion." The Declaration of the Church called it a "creative venture in interracial, intercultural, and interdenominational communion. In faith and genius it is Christian. While it derives its inspiration primarily from the source of Hebrew-Christian thought and life, it affirms the validity of spiritual insight wherever found and seeks to recognize, understand, and appreciate every aspect of truth whatever the channel through which it comes. It believes that human dignity is inherent in man as a creature of God, and it interprets the meaning of human life as essentially spiritual." Over the first few years, several versions of "the commitment" evolved, at first more Christian oriented, and then less so over time, reflecting in part Thurman's own move away from the Christianity of his youth and toward a more universal vision of cosmopolitan spirituality, humanitarianism, and what he called "sensitiveness." Thurman cultivated this by including in the church a meditation room with his own painting of Gandhi and various sacred texts.[31]

Thurman also used the church as a venue for experimentation

in worship aesthetics, especially music and dance. With the help of noted musician and arranger Corrine Williams, Thurman developed a music program at the church, later to be led by Raymond Fong. Thurman took pride in the choir as evidence of his ideas about worship as "the highest act of celebration of the human spirit," in which the "worshiper sees himself as being in the presence of God. In His presence, the worshiper is neither male nor female, black nor white, Protestant nor Catholic nor Buddhist nor Hindu, but a human spirit laid bare, stripped to whatever there is that is literal and irreducible." The key to the church was not the mixture of peoples but rather the "duality of the individual's religious experience achieved through worship and the effect of that experience on daily behavior." He saw Sunday morning as a time that, "for each person present," was "a moment which becomes *his* moment in the presence of God." This was consistent with Thurman's larger vision of churches as centers of spiritual nourishment, from which people could then be empowered to pursue social transformation.[32]

Eventually, Thurman moved the church out of the orbit of the Presbyterians. It became an independent congregation, subsidized in part by a national group of supporters (including Eleanor Roosevelt) and also by fees from Thurman's near-constant speaking engagements. Thurman lived on trains as much as he lived in the city itself. His star was in its ascendancy. He and the church were featured in *Life* magazine, and in 1953 he would be listed as one of the twelve most influential preachers in the country (at a time when such a list still had currency and still mattered). By that time also, he had become known for his book *Jesus and the Disinherited*, his most powerful work, and one that deeply influenced the thought of Martin Luther King Jr. Ironically, it was precisely that growing national prominence that made him the object of a number of tempting offers, including one from Boston University (BU), that eventually lured him back to the East Coast.

Thurman had grown the church to a congregation of about

250 members by the time he left in 1953. The president of Boston University wooed him away to become the first African American to serve as Dean of Marsh Chapel at BU. By that time, Thurman sensed his major work in San Francisco was at a point of transition, and he sought the opportunity to work again with students. He remained at BU until 1965. His time there was fraught with conflict, both with the president of the university, who had invited him there in the first place, and with seekers and experimenters in the early 1960s associated with Timothy Leary. Thurman protected his chapel's reputation from any implication with LSD experiments; Leary countered by casting Thurman as the sort of fogey who could not understand this new brand of consciousness seeking. Eventually Thurman concluded that LSD might expand consciousness, but it was an awfully expensive way to do so in comparison to his techniques of meditation, contemplation, and prayer.[30]

After retirement from BU and some further world travels in Africa and elsewhere, Thurman settled again in San Francisco, which was always his true spiritual home. His powerful mentorship drew people to him; he was the master of the art of the long, deep, searching conversation, the kind of talk that one hears well in his sermons. He published his later important work *In Search of Common Ground* in 1971, after the cresting and disillusioning of the hopes invested in the civil rights movement. Later in his life he became a revered senior mentor to a younger generation of black scholars, writers, and ministers. Howard Thurman lived out his days in San Francisco until 1981, writing his last books, creating the Howard Thurman Educational Trust, and compiling his papers, recordings, and addresses into an archive that is now available online and at the Howard Thurman Papers at BU.

MENTOR OF A MOVEMENT

Thurman served as one of the most influential philosophers and religious leaders of twentieth-century black America, a fact that only recently has become well understood. Thurman was a mentor of the civil rights movement, but he was not a movement man. That is, he educated a generation in precepts of nonviolence and a kind of internal transformation that would lead to a societal revolution, but he himself stayed in the background. "I have never considered myself any kind of leader," he later said. "I'm not a movement man. It's not my way. I work at giving witness in the external aspect of my life to my experience of the truth. That's my way—the way the grain in my wood moves."[34]

Of the many varied strands of Thurman's thought, a few highlight in particular his version of an African American religion born from the South but put in a global and cosmopolitan context. We may begin with his recovery of the meaning of the spirituals—one of Thurman's most original scholarly contributions, and something for which he is underappreciated. Not that he was first, or alone, in this, but he brought to the task a particular understanding of their meaning that differed from many others offered. Only W. E. B. Du Bois wrote about them with greater eloquence, and many in Thurman's era, who struggled to fit the spirituals into a social protest framework, therefore could not hear their poetry. Thurman could. Of the spirituals, he wrote, "There is no attempt to cast a false glow over the stark ruggedness of the journey. The facts of experience are seen for that they are—difficult, often even unyielding." What other people saw as otherworldly or escapist, he saw as precisely the point. The spirituals, he said, "made a worthless life, the life of a chattel property, a mere thing, a body, *worth living!* They yielded with abiding enthusiasm to a view of life which included all the events of their experience without exhausting themselves in those experiences. To them this quality of life was insistent fact because of that which deep within them, they discovered of God."[35]

Thurman's writings on the spirituals, produced in books such as *Deep River*, demonstrate a profound understanding of the various meanings and levels of what he saw as songs of survival—of inner endurance of an oppressed class. Much writing from that era cast the spirituals as a sort of protest music and overread specific directives into them. The so-called escapism, or otherworldliness, of the songs was in reality a "precious bane," he said, because "it taught people how to ride high to life, to look squarely in the face [of] those facts that argue most dramatically against all hope and to use those facts as raw material out of which they fashioned a hope that the environment, with all of its cruelty, could not crush. With untutored hands—with a sure artistry and genius created out of a vast vitality, a concept of God was wrenched from the Sacred Book, the Bible, the chronicle of a people who had learned through great necessity the secret meaning of suffering. This total experience enabled them to reject annihilation and affirm a terrible right to live." This was an extraordinary accomplishment, he suggested, because they brought out of sheer desperation an "infinite energy." They discovered God within themselves, and even as slaves they could live lives "worthy of the loftiest meaning of life." In the midst of circumstances bound to produce pessimism and despair, or a feeling that God was partial or even "demoniacal," they were never robbed of hope; they kept the hope that "the ultimate destiny of man is good." The songs were a "monument to one of the most striking instances on record in which a people forged a weapon of offense and defense out of a psychological shackle. By some amazing but vastly creative spiritual insight the slave understood the redemption of a religion that the master had profaned in his midst."[36]

Thurman's writings on the spirituals contrast but also pair with this reflections on mysticism. For Thurman, the root of human spirituality lay in a personal connection with God achieved through mystical experience; but for Thurman, such experiences made believers more, not less, connected to the everyday realities of the world. Thurman always attempted to balance his mysticism with activism and his reveries toward God with an emphasis on what should happen in this world because of that connection to God. This may be seen in his influence on what became the civil rights movement. He was, in many senses, the mentor of the movement. He spread the Gandhian gospel and planted the seeds of what would become the ethic of nonviolent resistance to white supremacy in America. He worked out his ideas, expressed later in *Jesus and the Disinherited*, that Jesus represented the oppressed in American society. Thurman had come to see, during the war, that segregation was in effect a will to dominate, and that it could only be defeated through powerful forces of resistance. His goal, as historians Peter Eisenstadt and Quinton Dixie explain, was to "rip people from their complicity and complacency with evil. Only in this way would people in power relinquish their hold on their place. It is not until something becomes movable in the situation that men are spiritually prepared to apply Christian idealism to un-ideal and un-christian situations." Full preparation to do nonviolent battle with Jim Crow, Thurman said, would require "great discipline of mind, emotions, and body to the end that forces may not be released that will do complete violence both to one's ideals and to one's purpose." [37]

Sitting in his class at Howard University in the late 1930s, where he was a divinity school student under Thurman's tutelage, James Farmer, soon to become one of the founding members of the Committee (later Congress) of Racial Equality (CORE), remembered penetrating philosophical questions, the point of which was to challenge students to think beyond becoming complicit in the American racial system of oppression. Born to a family of Texas Methodists, Farmer grew up witnessing the scars of segregation all around him and determined to do something when he could. With his training from Howard Thurman and others, Farmer became one of the founding members of CORE in Chicago in 1942. From its beginnings, Farmer later remembered, CORE determined that people, not experts or professionals, should lead the struggle for racial justice based on the principles of nonviolent direct action. CORE members helped to spread the practices of sit-ins in the 1940s. They initially focused their efforts on segregated institutions in

Chicago. The radical legacy of Thurman, Farmer, and CORE eventually found its way to the ministers and church communities in southern cities who began organizing boycotts and crusades early in the 1950s, leading up to Rosa Parks and the 381-day Montgomery bus boycott from 1955 to 1957. Later, Farmer and a group of others from CORE organized the Freedom Rides of 1961, when groups of integrated passengers boarded buses traveling through the Deep South, intending to test Supreme Court cases mandating segregation in interstate travel. The violence and bombings that met some of the travelers gripped the nation and dramatized the realities of segregation in the region. Two years later, Farmer involved himself in organizing the March for Jobs, Freedom, and Justice in Washington—now known as the March on Washington—when a quarter of a million people heard Martin Luther King deliver his most famous address. Thurman was there that day, and King's words rang for him as a poetic celebration of human unity. It was what Thurman had lived his life to envision and see in practice.

One of Thurman's most prominent intellectual mentees was Martin Luther King, who frequently quoted Thurman in his sermons. King frequently turned back to Thurman's classic *Jesus and the Disinherited*. In December 1955, at the beginning of the Montgomery bus boycott, King urged the crowd that the protests should be shaped by "the teachings of Jesus," that they must love their enemies, and concluded: "We, the disinherited of this land, we who have been oppressed so long, are tired of going through the long night of captivity. And now we are reaching out for the daybreak of freedom and justice and equality."[38]

Here, King was channeling Thurman, who spent much of his working life answering the question of what religion might mean for the dispossessed. "The masses of men live with their backs constantly against the wall. They are the poor, the disinherited, the dispossessed," Thurman wrote. And what did religion say to them? The answer to that question "is perhaps the most important religious quest of modern life." He answered it most fully in *Jesus and the Disinherited,* his classic from 1949, and his single most important written work. "The basic fact is that Christianity as it was born in the mind of this Jewish teacher and thinker appears as a technique of survival for the oppressed. That it became, through the intervening years, a religion of the powerful and the dominant, used sometimes as an instrument of oppression, must not tempt us into believing that it was thus in the mind and life of Jesus. . . . Wherever his spirit appears, the oppressed gather fresh courage; for he announced the good news that fear, hypocrisy, and hatred, the three hounds of hell that track the trail of the disinherited, need have no dominion over them."[39]

And he remained a critic of Christianity. "I belong to a generation that finds very little that is meaningful or intelligent in the teachings of the Church concerning Jesus Christ. . . . The desperate opposition to Christianity rests in the fact it seems, in the last analysis, to be a betrayal of the Negro into the hands of his enemies by focusing his attention upon heaven, forgiveness, love, and the like. . . . For years it has been a part of my own quest so to understand the religion of Jesus that interest in his way of life could be developed and sustained by the intelligent men and women who were at the same time deeply victimized by the Christian Church's betrayal of his faith." Thurman often retold the story of the slave minister who preached to the congregation including her grandmother: " 'You—you are not niggers. You—you are not slaves. You are God's children.' This established for them the ground of personal dignity, so that a profound sense of personal worth could absorb the fear reaction. This alone is not enough, but without it, nothing else is of value."[40]

Thurman's background as a black southern Christian formed the fundamental root of his philosophy, even when he had left behind that background. "A profound piece of surgery has to take place in the very psyche of the disinherited before the great claim of the religion of Jesus can be presented," he wrote. "Tremendous skill and power must be exercised to show to the disinherited the awful results of the role of negative deception into which their lives have been cast. How to do this is perhaps the greatest challenge that the religion of Jesus faces in modern life." Those in power attempt to keep the disinherited in fear for their lives and livelihood, because if they are able to get a greater vision, that of true liberty, then the "aim of *not being killed* is swallowed up by a larger and more transcendent goal." That is why it was so important to make the dispossessed feel like aliens, without any place in the social order.[41]

Thurman's work profoundly explored not only the psychology of relations between the powerful and the powerless but also the very fragility of the power held by authorities. It came, he suggested, with just a thin veneer covering over it: "The experience of power has no meaning aside from the other-than-self-reference which sustains it. If the position of ascendance is not acknowledged tacitly and actively by those over whom the ascendance is exercised, then it falls flat. Hypocrisy on the part of the disinherited in dealing with the dominant group is a tribute yielded by those who are weak. But if this attitude is lacking, or is supplanted by a simple sincerity and genuineness, then it follows that advantage due to the accident of birth or position is reduced to zero. Instead of relation between the weak and the strong there is merely a relationship between human beings. A man is a man, no more, no less. The awareness of this fact marks the supreme moment of human dignity."[42]

Thurman applied his theology directly to the effects of segregation. For him, any structure that presented the free flow of human beings into one another stifled the love ethic. And thus segregation or other means of separating humans constituted a "disease of the human spirit and the body politic," for the very existence of that separation "precludes the possibility of the experience of love as a part of the necessity of man's life." And love took work, because love for humanity as such did not exist: "There is no such thing as humanity. What we call humanity has a name, was born, lives on a street, gets hungry, needs all the particular things we need. As an abstract, it has no reality whatsoever." And that meant loving whole people, good and bad, including enemies. The key was to meet the person where they were, but to then treat the person as if they were already at the point where they could be reached. "Love demands that we expose ourselves at our most vulnerable point by keeping the heart open. Why? Because this is our own deepest need." We want to be treated not as the product of a single deed or mistake but as a integrated person, to be understood fully. "This is to have the experience of freedom, to be one's self, and to be rid of the awful burden of pretensions."[43]

Beyond his influence on particular sociopolitical movements, one may also examine Thurman's influence on the course of American theology, particularly in the area of mysticism. Thurman, drawing from Rufus Jones, made a distinction between passive and active mystics, and he was of the latter. Thurman the mystic always upheld the power of dreaming, to see visions of something different, beyond what was "realistic." "It is part of the pretensions of modern life to traffic in what is generally called 'realism,'" he once said. "There is much insistence upon being practical, down to earth. Such things as dreams are wont to be regarded as romantic or as a badge of immaturity, or as escape hatches for the human spirit." But, he added, "men cannot continue long to live if the dream in the heart has perished. It is then that they stop hoping, stop looking, and the last embers of their anticipations fade away. . . . Where there is no dream, the life becomes a swamp, a dreary dead place and, deep within, a man's heart begins to rot." The dream would not have to be "some great and overwhelming plan," but rather, could be the "quiet persistence of the heart that enables a man to ride out the storms of his churching experiences. . . . It is the touch of significance which highlights the ordinary experience, the common event." Thurman understood the presence of evil, but his emphasis was always on what was in the spirit of God in the world to overcome evil. The religious man would not be afraid of life, he said, because "he seeks at every point the emergence of the will and the mind of God from within himself and within the stuff of life itself. What is revealed in life is one with that which transcends life."[44]

Thurman carried on a tradition of those who found God in nature; in this way he drew from Henry David Thoreau and many others. At the same time, Thurman resisted being called a pantheist. Although it was true that God could be seen in nature, God could never be imprisoned in his own creation. Our bodies, he said, function as a whole; we do not become identified with a little finger or any other part. "The body is quite literally a dwelling place of the Most High God, Creator of the Universe." Human relations seem chaotic, often "more diabolical then benevolent." And yet amid the long history of human destruction, there always remained a will to create alternatives; there were always voices for peace amid war. And there were figures such as Gandhi, coming outside the Christian faith into an empire "whose roots were nurtured by that faith," and he became the embodiment of the intent to create other worlds, alternatives to human chaos and violence. "The moving finger of God in human history points ever in the same direction. There must be community."[45]

For Thurman, the "true purpose" of spiritual discipline was to "clear away whatever may block our awareness of that which is God in us. The aim is to get rid of whatever may so distract the mind and encumber the life that we function without this awareness, or as if it were not possible."[46] The hunger can take many forms and can be distorted and twisted, and yet it never disappears. "Prayer is the experience of the individual as he seeks to make the hunger dominant and controlling in his life. It has to move more and more to the central place until the hunger becomes the core of the individual's consciousness." As well, he emphasized the importance of the "moral essence of vital religious experience" in preparing "those

most engaged in sustaining democracy." Love of God and working to him would strengthen congregants to understand others;
they would become "apostles of sensitiveness," what we might call a
kind of mindfulness oriented towards social action.[47]

Thurman sought to recover the essential religious core of the
human experience and inculcate democratic habits of spiritually
grounded self-reliance. And he saw the church as a key resource for
those engaged in the creation of a just and loving society. For his
critics, Thurman's church was like a lemonade stand, where people
would pause to refresh themselves while on their way to somewhere
else. For Thurman, those people would not get to that "somewhere
else"—nor would society at large—without those moments of spiritual nourishment, those cool drinks on a hot day.

His quiet counsel to many provided that. "The greatest mystic-
ascetics in the Christian tradition have turned the whole stream of
Christian thought and achievement into new and powerful chan-
nels of practical living. It is basic to the Christian tradition that social sin and personal sin are bound up together in an inexorable relationship so that it is literally true that no man can expect to have
his soul saved alone," he wrote.[48]

Following his Quaker mentor in mysticism, Rufus Jones, Thurman declared himself an affirmation mystic, one who searched
spiritual experience in order to engage with the world more fully,
not to withdraw from it. Jones had said that the "mystic is always
more than any finite task declares," and yet he accepted the task because "he has discovered that only through the finite is the Infinite
to be found."[49] The finite could be an ordinary event of the day,
the beauty in nature, the deep engagement with another human
being, the pleasure of a well-cooked meal—any of it. Thurman advised, "Do not wait to hear His spirit winging near in moments
of great crisis, do not expect Him riding on the crest of a wave of
deep emotional excitement—do not look to see Him at the dra-
matic moment when something abnormal or spectacular is at hand.

Rather find Him in the simple experiences of daily living, in the normal ebb and flow of life as you live it."[50]

Another important truth of Thurman's was his ability to bring together different strands of the American religious tradition, that of individual transformation and social transformation. He connected the two in ways that deeply informed the Movement of the 1960s. He once wrote: "It seems to me that experience reveals a potent half-truth; namely, that the world can be made good if all the men in the world as individuals become good men. After the souls of men are saved, the society in which they function will be a good society. This is only a half-truth. Many men have found that they are caught in a framework of relationships evil in design, and their very good deeds have developed into instrumentalities for evil. It is not enough to save the souls of men; the relationships that exist between men must be saved also. To approach the problem from the other angle is to assume that once the relationships between men are saved, the individual men will thereby become instruments of positive weal. This is also a half-truth. . . . We must, therefore, even as we purify our hearts and live our individual lives under the divine scrutiny, so order the framework of our relationships that good men can function in it to the glory of God."[51]

HIS ULTIMATE INFLUENCE

"What made Thurman so valuable as a mentor and model for the nascent civil rights movement in the 1930s and 1940," one historian has explained, "was that he embraced his own contradictions, seeking the unity of God amid the bitter fractures and divisions of humanity; seeking an intensely spiritual and mystic religion, not as a refuge from the insistent responsibilities of the search for a better world, but as a way to realize it."[52]

Thurman always attempted to balance his mysticism with activism, his reveries toward God with an emphasis on what should happen in this world because of that connection to God. As well, he emphasized the importance of the "moral essence of vital religious experience" in preparing "those most engaged in sustaining democracy." As he told the *Christian Century* in 1973, "I didn't have to wait for the revolution. I have never been in search for identity, and I think that [all] I've ever felt and worked on and believed in was founded in a kind of private, almost unconscious autonomy that did not seek vindication in my environment because it was in me."[53] Love of God and working to him would strengthen us to understand others. Thurman's vision of the church emanated from that. As Thurman saw it, individuals in the thick of the struggle should have a place to "be able to find renewal and fresh courage in the spiritual resources of the church. . . . The true genius of the church was revealed by what it symbolized as a beachhead in society in terms of community, and as an inspiration to the solitary individual to put his weight on the side of a society in which no person need be afraid."[54]

Like all the figures discussed in the chapters of this book, Thurman's career contained many ironies and contradictions. Frank Price, a southern Presbyterian missionary, saw Chiang Kai-shek as the great hope for a democratic and socialist-leaning China; his religion of southern liberal Wilsonian internationalism was met with the hypernationalism of McCarthyism. In the next chapter, we will see three musical figures from the most provincial part of America, the Arkansas Delta, who ended up exercising perhaps the greatest influence of everyone discussed in this lecture series. They did so by fundamentally changing the sound of global popular music.

For Thurman, by contrast, the irony is that his universalist cosmopolitanism exercised its greatest influence on those who came specifically from the tradition of the African American church, whose internally focused and ethnically based churches then empowered the civil rights movement. And this happened in spite of the fact that Thurman was not well known then, and is even less known now, by a large number of African American religious leaders. His influence came from his deep well of intellectual thought, personal mentorship, and quiet prodding, far more than from any public role. Thurman's universalist vision eventually came to pass in the civil rights years in religious institutions that preached an idiomatic black American theology, and in ways that the leaders of those institutions often did not recognize. One of the aims of the Howard Thurman Papers Project and its corresponding institutions and research facility (also housed at Boston University), in fact, has been to make his work accessible to a generation who did not have personal contact with him and in many cases would not have studied him in universities or seminaries.

And yet ultimately Thurman moved history. He did so less through his creation of interracial visions, such as the Church for the Fellowship of All Peoples, but more through his translation of universalist ideas to an American religious idiom. Thurman was a "seeker" before we had such a term, and he paved the way for contemporary ideas of religious pluralism. In that sense, he really was (and is) America's pastor, as much if not more so than Billy Graham, because American religious ideals today look more like Thurman's than like Graham's. Thurman labored under anonymity, but ultimately the arc of history is bending his way.

The Blues and Gospel Train

Rosetta Tharpe, Johnny Cash, and the
Globalization of Southern Sounds

Johnny Cash loved Rosetta Tharpe, once calling her his favorite singer. The two grew up in the same neck of the woods in eastern/northeastern Arkansas: Tharpe in Cotton Plant and Cash in the experimental farming village of Dyess. Both yearned for bigger and greater worlds, and they discovered them. In the process, the music of southern Baptism and Pentecostalism hit the national stage. Consequently it shaped international perceptions of Americana and of what real American music was about. If Frank Price and Howard Thurman represented sets of ideas for transforming selves and societies, then Tharpe, Cash, and a host of others brought southern sounds to international stages. Ultimately, their versions of southern religion in global contexts proved to be the most influential of all.

There could hardly have been two more different people than Tharpe and Cash. The former was the exuberant and flamboyant carrier of a black gospel style, leavened with rhythm-and-blues guitar; the latter, the emblem of white country music and defender of the downtrodden. And both were completely distinct from their younger Arkansas compatriot Levon Helm, a native of Turkey Scratch, Arkansas (just down the road and a little east of Cotton Plant). He voiced characters from a mythical American past and thus gave life to songs usually written by others. By taking these three as emblems of the religion of southern music in global contexts, we can see how they shaped international perceptions. Many came before them, like their fellow Arkansan Sonny Boy Williamson and his generation of bluesmen. And many came after, including everyone from the Mississippian Sam Cooke and the Georgian James Brown to a lengthy list of others. The teaming of Tharpe, Cash, and Helm is thus somewhat accidental due to the regional conjunction of their birthplaces. In part, it's an artificial device to help narrow down the topic of the global reach of southern religious sounds. And yet, taking the three together moves us through a broad arc of southern sounds, both religious and secular. Such an approach will help us see why those sounds, originating in southern religious contexts and imagery, exercised such a global influence.

But here is the fundamental paradox of this topic. The sounds of the South, those that literally rocked the world in the mid-twentieth century and going forward, arose from a backward, reactionary, violent culture. By some equal and opposite force, artists from that region produced some of the most explosive popular music of the twentieth century.

From the nineteenth century to the present, southern musicians and those inspired by southern-born forms of music drew from biblical apocalyptic imagery, angry prophesy, gentle reassurances, and archetypical character struggles. They borrowed from a potent combination of extravagant biblical imagery, set within a fundamentalist culture of understanding and shaped by a violently inequitable social and economic system whose basic workings violated elementary biblical understandings of justice and fairness. These paradoxes collectively created the tensions that empowered the most memorably explosive music of American popular culture. The literalist biblical culture of the South inspired musical renderings of biblical texts that took their meanings far outside the confines of the readings sanctioned by the southern denominations.

That helps explain why a provincial culture, economically crippled by poverty and exploitation and intellectually straitjacketed by a biblical literalism and a suspicion of outside ideas and influences, produced a good deal of the "sound" of twentieth-century American culture. This sound eventually captured and shaped the popular music of much of the rest of the world. Far more certainly than the liberal Protestantism represented by Frank Price, and perhaps even more than the ecumenical ideas of the nonviolent philosophy transmitted from India to America via Howard Thurman and others, the sounds of the South turned out to exercise the greatest international influence. They exerted a disproportionate influence on the sound track of modernity as captured on record.[1]

Anyone who knew the recent history of the South hardly could have predicted it. Since the nineteenth century, the South was a problem. It was a region of slavery in a land of liberty, of economic backwardness in a land where people presumed perfection and aspired to progress, and of extralegal violence in a land of law and order. The region came to stand for everything that was backward—it represented futile energy and wasted lives stranded in a perversely unproductive economic system. Many perceived that southerners also seemed trapped in a religious worldview that sanctified the inequalities and exploitations of the economic system. A nascent southern liberal and radical movement sought to transcend the blues of southern history, but the participants faced entrenched injustices, inequalities, political torpor, and violence.

And yet, southern artistic geniuses blossomed during this period. From the early 1900s to the 1940s, southern cultural expressions, both in "low" and "high" arts, exploded. William Faulkner authored his groundbreaking modernist novels and Flannery O'Connor her stories exploring the southern grotesque; southern bluesmen created new forms of music that would reshape the country; black gospel writers penned some of the early classics of what would become the gospel music sound; vernacular visionaries such as Howard Finster and Sister Gertrude Morgan created works of great artistic intensity; and southern musicians flocked to record their songs and sermons for newly developing recording companies. Theatrical works celebrated the coming of modernity to the Tennessee Valley. Interracial cooperative farming and labor experiments at the Highlander Folk School in Tennessee and the Providence and Delta farms in Mississippi presaged alternatives to a region still portrayed through a moonlight-and-magnolias myth.[2]

Southern religious culture juxtaposed a pietist biblicism with wildly imaginative music, literature, and art. That striking contrast generated a productive tension between text-bound theology and the demands of artistic production. The literalistic biblical culture of the American South both inspired, but ultimately was overcome by, the spectacularly imaginative readings given to biblical passages by southern artists. In music, these came from the collectively anonymous authors of spirituals to the carefully rendered character sketches, ribald parodies, or angry manifestos of contemporary artists. Precisely by taking the Bible seriously as a literal and historical document, southern musicians extrapolated tales that wove their way into deeply American histories of struggle, injustice, triumph, backsliding, and visionary experiences.

A marriage of blues, country, gospel, soul, and jazz, all with deep roots in the South, constitutes the default sound of a good deal of American popular music, and certainly this was the case before the more recent rise of hip-hop. One major reason for this derives from the cultural intersections of race and southern Christianities. More than anyplace else, music in the religious South has deeply imprinted and shaped American life. In black spirituals, Americans learned of the deep theology and culture of the nation's most despised and oppressed people. Howard Thurman's pioneering works explored how those songs shaped the meaning making of generations of black slaves, teaching them about the value of their own lives while suggesting a realistic outlook on the limitations of those lives.[3] Through black and white variants of gospel music and the rhythmic intensity of black and white Pentecostalism during the twentieth century, Americans learned a spiritual dance. In the 1960s, spirituals morphed into freedom songs. Singers envisioned a new hope, and biblical imagery empowered movements for social change. In more contemporary forms of Americana, musical artists have returned to the kinds of biblical sketches of the folk musicians of decades ago, usually for the purpose of sketching out stories of mystery, irony, and tragedy. In all these cases, biblically inspired stories and meanings have stretched far beyond the kinds of restrictive renderings placed on biblical texts in the theology of the evangelical belt. Biblical tales, retold and spun into new forms, have inspired creative sound art for those who insisted that they needed nothing but the Bible but yearned for something more.

And that was the sound that transformed music internationally as well. Once picked up by English (and other European) hipsters and wannabe bluesmen and -women from the late 1950s, the music of the South went global. And when it did, it carried many of the religious visions of the region in the voices and instrumentations of black and white southerners. One can give a plethora of examples. For a full picture of the international influence of southern music, one would have to include the blues and secular forms, but that is not the purpose of this chapter. Here, the focus sharpens to Tharpe, Cash, and Helm, figures not normally considered together in this way (coming as they do from different genres and time periods of music). But in terms of a focus on southern religion and global context, these three stand as emblematic examples of the birth, origins, spread, and international impact of the sound of southern music and how that sound was secularized and globalized.

Coming from the most biblically grounded of cultures, those from the world of the Sanctified church (a generic term encompassing Holiness and Pentecostals generally) tapped into personal stories that spoke to archetypical themes that evoked a near-universal appeal. Black and white Pentecostals seized on the opportunities provided by mass media to spread their message. The influence of Holiness/Pentecostal performance styles broke through the stranglehold of "respectable" music that had defined southern bourgeois black services.

African American song styles dating from slavery fascinated listeners for their "strange," "weird," "primitive" melodic and rhythmic structures. But they dismayed many black church leaders who wanted to lead their congregations to sing more respectably. Part of the politics of respectability dating from the late nineteenth century was to displace African American styles of church music and assimilate those into a broad Protestant mainstream. But those musical forms deemed beyond the pale of respectability powered the revolutions of popular music in the twentieth century, both musically and lyrically.

Guitars, tambourines, and other rhythmical instruments, once seen as musical accompaniments for the devil, found their way into black Pentecostal churches in the early twentieth century. C. H. Mason's Church of God in Christ, the Memphis-based group that became the largest black Pentecostal denomination, immediately adopted them, and Tharpe grew up with those influences. Her mother served as an early evangelist for the church, and Rosetta joined her from a young age. White Pentecostalists soon picked them up, and the two shared hymns and holy dancing. White and black Pentecostal musical styles remained distinct, but they intersected at many points. Both employed rhythmical accompaniments, enthusiastic hollers, and holy dancing. Holiness and Pentecostal preachers and singers were among the most culturally innovative and entrepreneurial of twentieth-century plain folk southerners.

The first generation of rock music centrally featured southern performers. Aside from the obvious impact of the pioneering guitarist Rosetta Tharpe and performers such as Chuck Berry and Big Mama Thornton from the world of rhythm and blues, a generation of white southerners carried the music into the mainstream, even while retaining southern styles, accents, and musical influences. Jerry Lee Lewis, Carl Perkins, Charlie Rich, Johnny Cash, and of course Elvis married sacred and secular southern styles, as did black singers coming from Pentecostal and other evangelical churches. As the scholar Randall Stephens puts it, "hot music in the service of the Lord, believers assured themselves, was very unlike the riotous new rhythm and blues or rock and roll music. But they were more similar than the devout were willing to concede."[4] That's a wry understatement of the point. A biblically conservative culture could not contain its own text. In cultural production that played with the text, the extravagant imagery, metaphor, language, and poetry of the southern evangelical Bible inevitably took center stage.

In the twentieth century, Holiness and Pentecostal churches revivified nineteenth-century song. Holiness arose in the nineteenth century from a broad-based movement among Protestants to recapture the purity of the original church and move away from the formalized practices of American denominational religion. In the early twentieth century, Pentecostalism added to that movement its characteristic emphases on faith healing, speaking in tongues, and a complete capture of the soul by the Holy Ghost. As Pentecostals sought to restore the purity of the original church, they did so with a skillful use of the instruments of modernity, especially the broadcast media. The early saints intuitively mastered the world of electronic media. They also invented musical forms that revolutionized popular culture.

In the 1920s and 1930s, the birth of the recording music industry brought a new sort of musical education to ordinary southern folk. They purchased 78 RPM records put out by the Columbia, Okeh, and Paramount record companies. Meanwhile, the Bristol, Virginia, sessions of 1927 and the early Carter family recordings intermingled the sacred and the secular for white southern audiences. The recording industry grew up alongside, and made possible, rev-

olutions in popular music. These were recordings meant for segregated audiences, but they easily found their way to wider audiences through record sales and the radio. The earliest performers
prepared the way for the explosion of popular music to come in the
middle of the century when Cash and Tharpe made some of their
most important and influential recordings.

Recorded sermonizers rose to national prominence as did
bluesmen and -women, and through the same vehicle: the mass-
produced recording. Bluesmen and -women embodied the religious visions of moral ambiguity and outright evil. In this sense
they were religious figures, as quintessential as preachers. In profoundly personal ways, they explored the boundaries of the sacred
and the profane. Other performers wavered between their roles as
bluesmen and -women and preachers, unable fully to settle into either one but using that tension for memorable metaphorical explorations of the struggle within human souls.

A few decades later, when an Alabama-born preacher named
Elder Beck recorded "Rock and Roll Sermon," the lyrics of which
denounced rock as the devil's music, the preacher's guitar licks
rocked outrageously hard, undercutting (perhaps deliberately?) the
message. The way in which Elder Beck deconstructed his own text
provides a memorably powerful sonic example of the close connection but constant rivalry between the sacred and the secular
in twentieth-century African American popular music. Or maybe
Elder Beck was jealous of the success of Sister Rosetta.

SISTER ROSETTA

The entire line of black southern sacred music can be heard directly
in the life of the black gospel female pioneer Sister Rosetta Tharpe.
In the case of Tharpe, it was the sound of southern Pentecostalism set to the tuning of an electric guitar. The religious movements
of Holiness and Pentecostalism provided fertile ground for musical

interchange among white and black southerners and also provided the foundation for Sister Rosetta Tharpe and the birth of rock 'n' roll. Pentecostalism provided much of the soundtrack and expressive forms that reshaped American cultural styles later in the twentieth century. There is a straight line from Pentecostalism to gospel, soul, and rhythm and blues and through those into the heart of virtually all popular music that depends on a blue note, a back beat, and a religiously impassioned voice. The guitarist, singer, and performer kept alive the exuberant tradition of black religious music starting from the nineteenth century, continuing through the black gospel world of the twentieth, and eventually reaching into performances on stages, in nightclubs, and on records.

Born in Arkansas to a family active in the Sanctified church, Tharpe took the rhythmically expressive music of her upbringing and brought it to the world of street busking, revival tent singing, and later to the commercial marketplace of recordings and nightclubs. As a young girl, with her mother serving as a close associate and missionary for the Reverend Charles H. Mason's young Church of God in Christ (centered in the nearby city of Memphis), she stood on some boxes and belted out the song "Jesus Is on the Main Line." From that point forward, she rarely stopped performing in one venue or another, encompassing churches, nightclubs, concert halls, train stations, and television shows. Like many lyrics from that era, "Jesus Is on the Main Line" drew a spiritual moral from the use of a modern technology—hearers were urged to call up Jesus on the "main line" (the central line of a telephone system from that era) and "tell him what you want."[5] Her sacred passion, expressed most obviously in white and black southern Pentecostalism, was at the heart of R & B and rock 'n' roll.

Sister Rosetta was a guitarist of formidable chops who moved from street evangelism to performing gospel tunes at New York City's finest clubs and followed Dorsey in infusing popular tunes, blues feeling, and a nascent rhythm-and-blues sound into black

Protestant music. "Sister Rosetta Tharpe was anything but ordinary and plain," said Bob Dylan on his *Theme Time Radio Hour* show. "She was a big, good-lookin woman, and divine, not to mention sublime and splendid. She was a powerful force of nature. A guitar-playin', singin' evangelist."[6]

Cotton Plant and its surroundings was an incubator of musical talent, many coming from church backgrounds, but Rosetta was born shortly after the birth of the Church of God in Christ. In it, as scholar Gayle Wald writes, "modern black people, while reaffirming their essential dignity through Holiness living, might do so without abandoning the sustaining religious practices of the past." The church embraced the "pleasures of communal singing and dance as expressions of faith." The heavy influence of women in gospel meant that women were key to the birth of rock as well, despite its masculine image. And Rosetta's facility in wielding her guitar as a weapon of sound, pleasure, and authority was at the bottom of that.[7]

So was her performance style. In later years, when she raised her hands above her head in performance, she recalled Church of God in Christ (COGIC) doctrine urging the use of the outstretched arms in prayer; when she put a little swing in her spirituals, she echoed COGIC's liberal approach to blues. The Pentecostal Church provided her with her first audiences, and even after she was in exile from it, she carried its message in song.

Accompanying herself on guitar, at first as a solo act and later with larger groups and jazz bands, Tharpe soon drew renown for her musical chops with her ax. Traveling through the country in the 1920s and 1930s, Tharpe served as a music evangelist first alongside her mother (a preacher for the COGIC) and then with her husband. Like blues instrumentalists, Tharpe picked her guitar with an insistently rhythmic one-note sound that accompanied a large variety of religious lyrics drawn from all eras of American sacred music. The style was a staple of numerous other street performers and evangelists, including Blind Lemon Jefferson and Blind Willie

Johnson. In the later 1930s, Tharpe traveled to New York, played with Benny Goodman and Cab Calloway, and appeared in John Hammond's famous "From Spirituals to Swing" concerts at Carnegie Hall. As a young performer, she instinctively sensed the future of the fusion of gospel and popular styles, the music that would shape the sound of the world later in the century. Her Cotton Club performance in 1938 transported her to celebrity status even as it discomfited a portion of her Sanctified audience. From there, Tharpe produced numerous recordings for the Decca record company. "She sings in a night club because she feels there are more souls in the nighteries that need saving than there are in church," a black newspaper reported of her choice to bring jazzy guitar sound and gospel lyrics to New York nightlife. Tharpe's ready transition from the world of Sanctified religion to the market of popular religious recordings traced a path that brought black religious music to a popular mainstream audience through the course of the twentieth century.[8]

For performers such as Tharpe, a gulf stretched between music industry expectations and gospel ones. As a young woman, Tharpe and others in her orbit "had used their individual talents to testify to the power of the divine in their lives and to convey that power to others." But those kinds of spiritual longings were an uncomfortable fit in a music industry interested in charisma and sexual appeal more than in musical abilities. Tharpe had to adjust to that corporate milieu and set of conventions. In doing so, she took important lessons from New York bandleaders, who groomed her for the theatrical world.[9]

Tharpe was often compared to Mahalia Jackson, the gospel singer who first broke out in the 1930s with her earliest recording "God's Gonna Separate the Wheat from the Tares," a recording that still jumps out and astounds the listener.[10] Jackson's celebrity developed around her reputation as a defender of gospel tradition, while Rosetta earned notoriety for her instinct for creative insubordination and her practiced talent for showbiz flamboyance, spiritual singing that could bust out in blues cadences, and her guitar virtuosity.

Tharpe also represented a key move made by so many of the musical pioneers. She resisted the moral severity of the Pentecostal Church but embraced its emotional exuberance. She saw her talents as coming from the divine and believed she was doing God's work as a popular musician. As the gospel scholar Horace Boyer puts it, "Sister did more than anyone else in introducing the music of the Negro church to the world."[11]

As one contemporary remembered her, "It was just her singing and her picking that guitar that just drew. You just got attached to it. She could really hit that, now. . . . You can sing, and it's a beautiful voice, and everything, but if you sing with an *understanding* and the feeling of what you're singing it's altogether different. And that is what she did, more like to me. Even though she was young. It was a gift. Yes." Rosetta made the guitar an extension of her body. She let her instrument speak through her. The way her guitar talked paralleled the act of speaking in tongues, serving as a symbol of the authenticity of possession by the Holy Spirit. "Where did rock and roll come from? It came from the music of the Negro Churches, definitely," noted Pearl Bailey. Rosetta could play with abandon but control; her playing revealed "the art of the guitar as an instrument of ineffable speech, of rapture beyond words." Rosetta played the guitar like she owned it. Even in moments of performance when she was in possession of the Holy Ghost spirit, she possessed the instrument with electrifying physicality.[12]

Her gift was evident in her first big hit that produced her characteristic sound of gospel becoming rhythm and blues, "Strange Things Happening Every Day," released just at the end of World War II in Europe. Tharpe directed her lyrics (available at https://www.lyrics.com/lyric/1577220/Strange+Things+Happening+Every+Day) at those from her Pentecostal background who could not accept her move into secular venues, even though she was bringing church sounds into those places. Church people might claim to be in a "holy way," but in fact there were "strange things happening every day."

The song speaks to living in a world where the unexpected can happen anytime, including anything from the hypocrisy of church people to Jesus healing the blind. Its popularity initially peaked in 1945, then it developed a second life in the mid 1950s when it exerted a strong influence on Sun Studios and the white music producer Jim Dickinson. A few years later Rosetta toured with the Jordanaires, a white quartet whose members admired Rosetta's work ethic and her business savvy. She also appeared as a kind of proxy for the black church in the Grand Ole Opry in 1947, singing together with black gospel greats the Fairfield Four.

Through these years, she influenced the young men who would soon go on to create the sounds of rock 'n' roll, but the very success of those performers soon eclipsed Rosetta as a star in America. By the late 1950s, she had to seek out new audiences abroad, and she found them first in England. Her first London appearance in late 1957 was at the Chiswick Empire Theater, where she played to a sellout crowd. The rebirth of her career started when Chris Barber, leader of England's most popular traditional jazz band, invited her on a three-week, twenty-city British tour for $28,500. Dates soon followed for her in France, Monte Carlo, Germany, Denmark, Sweden, and Switzerland. These tours rejuvenated her and showed that God would lift you up.[13]

From then until 1970, just as her time of stardom descended in America, eclipsed by the younger generation who learned many of the tricks of the trade from her, Rosetta was a hit in Europe. Young Brits admired Rosetta's innovative use of electric guitar as a solo instrument with its own distinctive power of speech. She taught those audiences the arts derived from her church training: how to warm up a congregation/audience, bring it to shouting, and then cool it down. "But Rosetta had managed to render the preacher's routine in her staged performances, introducing European listeners to a kind of secular rapture," her biographer writes. Rosetta's playing pioneered the electric guitar as the lead rock instrument, and she became one of the lead performers in giving a global reach to southern religious sounds. "Blues is just the theatrical name for gospel," she told Val Wilmer in 1960, "and true gospel should be slow, then hands clap and that's jubilee or revival, and then you get a little happier and that's jazz . . . and then you make it like rock 'n' roll." Or, as she told the London *Daily Mirror*, "All this new stuff they call rock 'n' roll, why, I've been playing that for years now."[14] As Gayle Wald explains it:

> No other American woman was as central to the transatlantic flow of sound that we know today as the British Invasion as Sister Rosetta Tharpe. A woman among men and a gospel musician among secular blues players she was still somewhat sidelined as an anomaly. Paradoxically, however the very qualities that had always rendered Rosetta an outsider—her flamboyance, her over the top style, her association with the guitar, her need to differentiate herself from other performers through unconventional choices and outrageous behavior—rendered her irresistibly compelling to the British blues-rockers of the 1960s.[15]

Tharpe's international influence reached another peak in the Blues and Gospel Train event of 1964, set strangely in a train station outside Manchester. The performers appeared on one side, suffering through a dismal, cold, and rainy English day, and the audience observed on the other. Sister lit up the crowd with her hits and showed the others, including acts such as Muddy Waters, how it was done. Strangely, in spite of the much-heralded folk revival in America, that same tour had only one stop at Hunter College in New York City. Sister Rosetta had years to come performing abroad, where she became a star, but she was on her way to being forgotten in America—a forgetting that only recently has been rectified. As the scholar Gayle Wald sums it up, "Whenever a rock or gospel or rhythm-and-blues musician turns the amps up, we're in the living presence of Rosetta, who made a habit of playing as loud as she could, based on the Pentecostal belief that the Lord smiled on those who made a joyful noise."[16]

JOHNNY CASH

Johnny Cash saw Sister Rosetta in 1960 and later described it as one of the most moving musical experiences of his life. Rosetta was the musician he admired the most. Cash was twenty years younger than Sister but born in the same general milieu, and he was influenced by the same sounds of the religious South and the secular world. He was part of a generation of young men around Memphis in the mid-1950s who caught the spark of the blues sound and brought it to a larger audience, including white country audiences. Before seeing her, Cash generally had followed Tharpe's career and noted the way she brought gospel sound to secular venues and married the two forms in powerfully new musical creations. He hoped to do the same.[17]

Sacred passion, expressed most obviously in white and black southern Pentecostalism, was at the heart of rhythm-and-blues and rock'n' roll. That sacred passion was not protection enough against descents into self destruction or impulses to enjoy the pleasures of the flesh. Both the more sentimental music of southern evangelicalism and the tunes of southern hard religion come through in the career of Johnny Cash. The persona of the man in black embodied a darkness that symbolized both his own Christlike identification with the poor and downtrodden in society and his constant struggle with personal demons. Cash's recordings follow a trajectory well-known to southerners, and especially to bluesmen and -women, as they struggled within themselves between good and evil impulses.

In Dyess, Arkansas, an experimental community created by a New Deal agency to resettle white farmers displaced by the agricultural crises of the Depression, Cash started carrying water to families in the fields as a young boy. JR, as he was known, followed radio singers like others followed baseball. He often lingered to sing gospel with them, and he joined family times in the evening with a guitar or an upright piano, singing from a Baptist hymnbook. "In future years when overwhelmed by drugs and other pressures," his biographer Robert Hilburn writes, "he would often isolate himself and turn to music as a refuge, the purity of music was a place of comfort and affirmation." And gospel was key. Another biographer writes:

> Gospel songs he sang in church, at home, and in the fields, numbers such as "I'll Fly Away" and "Life's Evening Sun," told about Jack's destiny and Christ's promise of renewal and hope. Gospel music, more than revival meetings, preachers, and Sunday school classes, propped up the boy as he walked along. Dispatches from God, the songs filtered into his being where they remained for the rest of his life, never falling away from his repertoire. Few secular songs learned in his youth traveled so well.[18]

JR (he became "Johnny" in the 1950s) grew up listening to black artists on the radio from Memphis, and over time he wove together more rootsy influences with what he gathered from others, including black singers. One of his favorites was Sister Rosetta, no longer by then an Arkansan but one who left a long legacy behind her. Cash had followed her career, "admiring the way she mixed gospel themes with a rollicking, high-energy blues style—as on 'Strange Things Happening Every Day.' In time he learned that she took spiritual music into nightclubs and dance halls, not just churches and stately auditoriums—something he hoped to do one day." Cash learned also from watching services at the Church of God (Cleveland), a white Pentecostal denomination. He remembered the scenes of religious ecstasy there, including the "writhing on the floor, the moaning, the trembling, and the jerks." The powerful sermons and polyphonic music also impressed him.[19]

Johnny had a history of personal racism, which he later freely acknowledged, and was abusive to some he served with while he was in the U.S. Air Force in Germany. But he grew out of that, and early in his career he was recording folk and blues from Big

Bill Broonzy, Memphis Slim, and Sonny Boy Williamson that spoke about brutal racism in the South. His time in Germany, and later performances for the USO, gave him some of his first chances abroad; he felt blessed, with good fortune that God was watching over him and that he could be going through some form of redemption.

"Ring of Fire," one of Johnny's earliest hits, was for him what "Strange Things Happening Every Day" was for Sister Rosetta—a breakthrough hit that ambiguously straddled the world of the sacred and the secular. He once described the song as "my first gospel hit" and said of it, "I'm going to be true not only to those who believe in me and depend on me, but to myself and God—a song that might give courage to others as well as myself."[20]

This led to the Folsom State Prison recording of 1968. Cash carried with him an identification with those in opposition to authority; his own occasional experiences with the legal system only reinforced that attitude. He carried this identification to what became his epic live recording in Folsom State Prison in 1968, *At Folsom Prison*, an album that remains an American classic from the era. At a meeting prior to the recording of the album, someone challenged him: "Your fans are church folk, Johnny. Christians. They don't want to hear you singing to a bunch of murderers and rapists tryin' to cheer them up." Cash responded: "Well they're not Christians then."[21]

Throughout his career, Cash felt called to return to recording gospel music and hymns, often just after making successful commercial recordings of his hits. Thus, after "I Walk the Line" in 1957, he signed with Columbia Records, put on his first album Dorothy Love Coates's "That's Enough," and recorded another entire album of hymns. Likewise, after the Folsom State Prison recordings came his *Gospel Road* project, a labor of love for which he never recouped his very large personal investment of time and money. And he concluded his life with *My Mother's Hymn Book*, saying of it, "The songs in that old book mean more to me than I can tell you, so I'll just sing 'em, me and my guitar, simple, no adornment, knowing that God loves music and that music brings hope for a better tomorrow."[22]

Through the 1970s, Cash careened between evangelical commitment and drug problems, the dichotomy that defined him and, strangely enough, made him more authentic (in spite of what might have been seen as hypocrisy among other people). He immediately hit it off with Billy Graham; they bonded like brothers despite having an age difference of fourteen years. Billy's son told him Cash could attract people to crusades. Cash told him "how fulfilled gospel music made him feel, that he had never been more inspired to write a song than when he wrote He Turned the Water Into Wine." They first appeared together in 1970 in Knoxville, and Graham said that he saw the preacher in Johnny: "You heard it in his testimony and listened to it in his music. June encouraged that preacher in him as well." Around this time Cash publicly professed his faith and joined the Evangel Temple Church in Hendersonville, Tennessee, an Assembly of God (Pentecostal) congregation that practiced the baptism of the Holy Spirit and speaking in tongues. Johnny followed that up with his film *Gospel Road: A Story of Jesus* and accompanying album *The Gospel Road* in the early 1970s, in which the man in black strolled around the Holy Land while a Swedish actor, playing Jesus, reenacted the biblical stories of Jesus's life (with June Carter Cash appearing as Mary Magdalene, playing her as someone with both an emotional and an erotic attraction to Jesus). The film, writes Cash's biographer Michael Streissguth, "proved a compelling personal statement and a credible interpretation of Christ's days on earth, if one could look past the sharp Southern accent of Mary Magdalene and the preponderance of comb-overs among males in the cast." Cash's Jesus is a very human divine figure, walking among humans and in the landscape "as if He were of it, not above it." Meanwhile, he appeared as a headliner at Explo '72, one of the first Christian rock festivals in the country (sometimes called Godstock), and from there he released a number of straight gospel albums. By this point, Johnny's fame had grown abroad, and he recorded a live album at the London Palladium, joined by the Tennessee Three and the Carter Family, covering high points in career.[23]

His music career struggled, though, and one music executive told him he should stop going to church and start going back to prisons. He made popular gospel albums, including a remake of Sister Rosetta Tharpe's "This Train Is Bound for Glory," popularized in the 1930s by his longtime favorite. In fact, Cash would often describe Tharpe as his favorite singer—not favorite gospel singer but favorite singer, period. He brought in black gospel singers from Tennessee State, and later recorded other songs written by or associated with Tharpe. As his biographer explains, "the edgy mix of sacred and sensual in Tharpe's music made him think briefly about devoting half of the album to her songs, or maybe even to use the entire album to showcase black gospel music."[24]

Later in the 1970s he made another European tour and became a sort of adopted national singer in Ireland. He appeared also with Carl Perkins, Marty Stuart, and others in another European tour, attempting to re-create the sound of the Million Dollar Quartet. Touring with him for the first time, Marty Stuart saw that Johnny had rock star energy: "He brought a higher level of energy and confidence to the European shows. People always talked about how he prowled the stage with the electricity of a panther in the 1960s, but this was the first time I saw it and it was great being onstage with him." Later, the star of U2, Bono, said that Cash was a "quintessential character of the scriptures, or at least the characters in the Bible that interested me." Flawed characters like David, Jacob, "wild blokes."[25]

Cash's recordings toward the end of his life, collected in a five-volume *American Recordings* set, allowed him ample space to explore his lifelong mutually contradictory passions. In his music, Jesus appears as a figure of lightness and grace, but "the beast in me" is more than powerful enough to overcome and simply snuff out His presence on earth. Cash expressed an older culture of a hard religion that spoke of the blood of Jesus coming from his hands and side, his blood giving life and setting captives free. This was a hard religion of white and black southerners that found expression from pioneering bluesman Charley Patton's "Prayer of Death" (from the early 1930s) to Johnny Cash's recordings of late classics such as "Redemption Song" and "Personal Jesus." This was a personal Jesus of suffering southerners from both sides of the color line.[26]

Starting with the name "Johnny," Cash was a performer, an artist, someone around whom myths and legends grew. And yet, like Tharpe, he radiated authenticity. They were performers whose very stage characters emerged from their authentic selves. Of Cash, one author writes (and it could be said of Tharpe as well), "He actively participated in the making of a cultural icon that had, and continues to have, vast significance for many people . . . thereby filling this iconic image of Johnny Cash with real, authentic value." By embracing the identity given to him, Cash lived in a way that made his stage character something more than an "externally imposed persona." Like Tharpe, Cash breathed authentic life into his stage persona, because being front and center on stage was his life, his calling, and his pleasure.[27]

LEVON HELM

The story of the great drummer, singer, and actor Levon Helm varies from the others, because Helm did not come from the kind of religious background that Cash and Tharpe did. And he was not personally the vehicle of religious expression in the way the other two were. Rather, he became a vehicle for the American collective consciousness represented in The Band. He was also a symbol for The Band's chief songwriter, the Canadian Robbie Robertson, who wrote songs about southern wanderers, vagabonds, and searchers that he could express in the voice of Helm. The result was a short-lived period of musical magic that once was called "country soul," a label Helm hated but that in fact was fairly apt. Nowadays we might just call it Americana, splashed with a dose of Dylan-esque surrealism and some bluesy rock 'n' roll as well. "The only songs that we do in relation to the South at all are sung by Levon," Robertson told *Melody Maker* in 1971, "and I write those songs for the people who sing them. Richard and Rick don't sing about the South; it works for Levon because he's from Arkansas. We're not doing something that we don't know nothing about. I'm trying to write songs that he could sing, lyrics that he can get off on—like 'The Night They Drove Old Dixie Down.'"[78]

What Helm did for The Band was supply them with one of the great drummers of the twentieth century along with a voice that was steeped in the rhythms, sounds, and accents of the South. The Band provided Helm with song vehicles to carry southern dreams as well as to serve as a symbol of southern and American religions writ onto a larger stage. It's little wonder that, when *Music from Big Pink* arrived in 1969, Eric Clapton decided he wanted to quit a massive blues-rock band like Cream and join The Band. Clapton and many others were drawn to authenticity, and Helm had that. From there, Helm took his act to the movies, as the father of Loretta Lynn in *Coal Miner's Daughter*, and later he carried on and basically *was* Americana music at his midnight rambles in New York until his death in 2012.

But consider what Helm conveyed in his voicing of classics such as "Night They Drove Old Dixie Down," where he becomes an ordinary dirt farmer Confederate, straggling through the end of the war, and reflecting a farmer's perception of a world where hard work might be of small gain: "Well I don't mind choppin' wood, and I don't care if the money's no good, you can take what you need and leave the rest." And then the worship of Lee: "But they should never have taken the very best." The other best-known song of The Band, "The Weight," features a strange patched-together tune full of contemporary real people turned into mythic figures, which then becomes an anthem and a contemporary hymn. "The Weight" follows a traveling character, a pilgrim, and the possible interpretations of his encounters with the other characters could multiply with every listener. As one explicator puts it:

> The song is most simply about the burdens we all carry. The "weight" is the load that we shoulder when we take on responsibility or when we try to do good. But it's also the heaviness that presses down on us when we fall into "sin" or wrestle with "temptation." It's a song about a universally human dilemma. But, just as the writers drew from their own pasts in fleshing out their cast, it's conceivable that they also drew from their own experiences in conceptualizing the "weight." Perhaps the song refers to the very real loads shouldered by Band members, the very real burdens that resulted from the good and the bad in their own lives.[29]

By the time we get to Levon Helm, we're out of the kind of explicit religiosity seen in many predecessors and into a world of mythic religiosity featuring characters in songs as both real figures and archetypes drawn from real life, cinema, and fantasies. Helm became the carrier of the dreams of southern music and religion. He was the kind of character that someone like Bob Dylan could draw from and draw energy from. And from him we later move into the world of Wilco, of Gillian Welch, of Valerie June, of so many others who turn songs into archetypical explorations of a mystic, and mythic, religiosity emanating from the South.

From the nineteenth century to the present, then, southern musicians and those inspired by southern-born forms of music drew from biblical apocalyptic imagery, angry prophesy, gentle reassurances, and archetypical character struggles. The potent combination of the biblically poetic, set within a literalist scriptural understanding and juxtaposed to a violent and inequitable social and economic system, collectively created the tensions that empowered the most memorably explosive music of American popular culture.

Southern visual and oral vernacular artists inspired musical ren-derings of biblical texts, which took their meanings far outside the confines of the readings sanctioned by the southern denominations. The tensions contained within the culture, expressed through mu-sic, helped to vault southern performers such as Cash and Tharpe to stardom and created character songs memorably voiced by cre-ative artists such as Helm. And sometimes, as in the case of Cash, those tensions and ambitions drove addictions that could destroy lives. At the same time, the music also provided one means of the coming southern cultural and political revolution.

The list of southern performers with religious backgrounds or connections who fed the globalization of southern sounds could go on. Here, the artificial conceit of three very different perform-ers and personalities, who happen to come from the same general region of Arkansas, demonstrates the essential point about south-ern popular religion that set a global context for the popularization and proliferation of a certain sound. The sounds of the South be-came a part of the soundtrack of the globe in ways few could have imagined in an earlier era when the region seemed to be a hope-less backwater. With regards to cultural production, no place could be seen as more important. In the twentieth century, southerners shaped the soundtrack of the globe.

NOTES

CHAPTER I.
LOST IN TRANSLATION

1. Kristopher C. Erskine, "Frank W. Price, 1895–1974: The Role of an American Missionary in Sino-U.S. Relations" (PhD diss., University of Hong Kong, 2013), 402. Erskine's dissertation, which I discovered after doing much of the primary source research for this chapter, is an outstanding work that provided much-needed background for this part of my work.

2. David Hollinger, *Protestants Abroad: How Missionaries Tried to Change the World but Changed America* (Princeton: Princeton University Press, 2017).

3. In "Frank W. Price, 1895–1974," Erskine discusses his stymied efforts to gain access to the government's classified Price files.

4. Erskine, "Frank W. Price, 1895–1974," 195.

5. Stephen G. Craft, "American Isaiah in China: Frank W. Price, Chiang Kai-Shek and Reforming China, 1941–1949," *Journal of Presbyterian History* (2004): 18; Frank W. Price, *China—Twilight or Dawn?* (New York: Friendship Press, 1948), 20.

6. Chiang Kai-Shek, "My Religious Faith," address delivered April 16, 1938, reprinted in *The China Reader*, vol. 2, ed. Franz Schurman (New York: Random House, 1967), 154–57, available also at http://www.olemiss.edu/courses/inst203/chiang38.pdf.

7. Laymen's Foreign Mission's Inquiry, Chairman William Ernest Hocking et al., *Rethinking Missions: A Laymen's Inquiry after One Hundred Years* (New York: Harper & Brothers, 1932).

8. *Rethinking Missions*, 37.

9. Bae Kyounghan, "Chiang Kai-Shek and Christianity: Religious Life Reflected from His Diary," *Journal of Modern Chinese History* 3 (2009): 1–10.

10. Ibid.

11. Xi Lian, *Redeemed by Fire: The Rise of Popular Christianity in Modern China* (New Haven: Yale University Press, 2010), 243.

12. Typescript labeled "Chiang Kai-Shek," summaries of speeches from 1934 to 1945, found in Frank W. Price Papers, George W. Marshall Library, Lexington, Virginia, Box 2, folders 10–12 (hereafter FWP); Xi Lian, *Redeemed by Fire: The Rise of Popular Christianity in China* (New Haven: Yale University Press, 2010), 119.

13. Chiang Kai-Shek, "Fight to Win," October 9, 1937, from Nanking; Address on Nov. 17, 1941; "A New World Built on Christian Love," December 25, 1942; all reprinted in *Resistance and Reconstruction: Messages during China's Six Years of War, 1937–1943* (New York: Books for Libraries Press, 1943), 24, 268, 318.

14. Craft, "American Isaiah in China," 181.

15. "Christmas Eve Broadcast to Wounded and Sick Soldiers," December 24, 1943, translated by Frank Price, typescript in FWP.

16. Chiang Kai-Shek, *The Collected Wartime Messages of Generalissimo Chiang Kai-Shek, 1937–1945*, vol. 1 (New York: John Day, 1943).

17. Ibid.

18. Paul A. Varg, *Missionaries, Chinese, and Diplomats: The American Protestant Missionary Movement in China, 1890–1952* (Princeton: Princeton University Press, 1958), 255.

19. Erskine, "Frank W. Price, 1895–1974," 405.

20. Price to Madame Chiang, April 14, 1941, in FWP; Stephen G. Craft, "American Isaiah in China: Frank W. Price, Chiang Kai-Shek and Reforming China, 1941–1949," *Journal of Presbyterian History* (2004): 180–203.

21. Meiling Soong Chiang to Dr. R. J. MacMullen, from Chungking, Szechuan, March 3, 1941, FWP; H. Maxcy Smith to Madame Chiang Kai-Shek, April 8, 1941, FWP.

22. Price to Madame Chiang, December 9, 1941, in FWP.

23. Letter from Price to Gen. and Madame Chiang, from Nanking Theological Seminary in Chengtu, August 27, 1943, in FWP.

24. Craft, "American Isaiah in China," 190; Memo from Price to Chiang Kai-Shek, undated [December 5, 1944], in FWP; Chiang Kai-Shek to Frank Price, December 15, 1944, in FWP.

25. Letter from Price to Gen. and Madame Chiang, from Nanking Theological Seminary in Chengtu, August 27, 1943, in FWP.

26. Price to Chiang Kai-Shek, from Shanghai, June 23, 1946, in FWP; Craft, "American Isaiah," 197–98.

27. Price to Chiang Kai-Shek, from Shanghai, June 23, 1946, in FWP; Craft, "American Isaiah," 197–98.

28. "Letter to Generalissimo," August 21, 1945, in FWP.

29. Craft, "American Isaiah," 195.

30. Telegram from Madame Chiang Kai-Shek to Frank Price, December 23, 1945, in FWP; Price to Madame Chiang Kai-Shek, January 21, 1947, in FWP; and typescript from *New York Herald Tribune*, January 11,1947, in FWP; Madame Chiang to Price, from Nanking, February 1947, FWP.

31. Erskine, "Frank W. Price, 1895–1974," 505–16.

32. Harrison, "Communism and Christianity," 96, 103, 118–20.

33. Stephen Harrison, "Communism and Christianity: Missionaries and the Communist Seizure of Power in China" (PhD diss., Vanderbilt University, 2013); Phillip L. Wickeri, *Seeking the Common Ground: Protestant Christianity, the Three-Self Movement, and China's United Front* (Eugene, Oreg.: Wipf & Stock, 2011), 7–8, 136–37.

34. Erskine, "Frank W. Price, 1895–1974," 590.

35. Frank Price, *Marx Meets Christ* (Philadelphia: Westminster Press, 1957), 13, 17, 29, 74.

36. Allen Licthman, *White Protestant Nation: The Rise of the American Conservative Movement* (New York: Grove Press, 2009), 154.

37. Wickeri, *Seeking the Common Ground*, 121.

38. Jay Taylor, *The Generalissimo: Chiang Kai-Shek and the Struggle for Modern China* (Cambridge, Mass.: Harvard University Press, 2011), 432, 456.

CHAPTER 2.
THE MEANING OF ALL HIS STRIVINGS

The epigraph is from Howard Thurman, *For the Inward Journey: The Writings of Howard Thurman*, selected by Anne Spencer Thurman (Richmond, Ind.: Friends United Meeting, 1984), 237.

1. Quinton Dixie and Peter Eisenstadt, *Visions of a Better World: Howard Thurman's Pilgrimage to India and the Origins of African American Nonviolence* (Boston: Beacon Press, 2011); Gary Dorrien, *Breaking White Supremacy: Martin Luther King and the Black Social Gospel* (New Haven: Yale University Press, 2017); Peter Eisenstadt, *Against the Hounds of Hell: A Life of Howard Thurman* (forthcoming 2020 from University of Virginia Press); *The Papers of Howard Washington Thurman*, ed. Walter Fluker et al. (Columbia: University of South Carolina Press, 2008–2019). Information on *The Psalm of Howard Thurman* may be found at *http://www.howardthurmanfilm.com/*, and on *Backs against the Wall: The Howard Thurman Story*, at *http://journeyfilms.com/howardthurman*. For invaluable primary source material, including digitized recordings of Thurman's sermons and addresses, researchers

should consult the Howard Thurman and Sue Bailey Thurman Collections at Boston University at http://archives.bu.edu/web/howard-thurman/howard-thurman-collection.

2. This story is told in various places, including in Paul Harvey, "Meet the Theologian Who Helped MLK See the Value of Nonviolence," *The Conversation*, January 11, 2018, https://theconversation.com/meet-the-theologian-who-helped-mlk-see-the-value-of-nonviolence-89938. Links are provided there to various of the quotations and incidents noted below.

3. Howard Thurman to Albert W. Dent, December 14, 1954, in Walker Earl Fluker, ed., *The Papers of Howard Washington Thurman*, 4 vols. (Columbia: University of South Carolina Press, 2009–18), 4:98.

4. Howard Thurman, *Jesus and the Disinherited* (orig. 1949; reprint ed., Boston: Beacon Press, 1976).

5. A shorter version of this story, told in more detail in *Vision of a Better World*, may be found at Quinton Dixie and Peter Eisenstadt, "When Howard Thurman Met Mahatma Gandhi: Nonviolence and the Civil Rights Movement," Beacon Broadside online, http://www.beaconbroadside.com/broadside/2014/10/when-howard-thurman-met-mahatma-gandhi-nonviolence-and-the-civil-rights-movement.html.

6. https://www.bu.edu/today/2011/who-was-howard-thurman/; see also Walter Fluker, "Dangerous Memories and Redemptive Possibilities: Reflections on the Life and World of Howard Thurman," in *Black Leaders and Ideologies in the South: Resistance and Non-Violence* (New York: Routledge, 2005), 147–76.

7. http://www.pbs.org/wnet/religionandethics/2002/01/18/january-18–2002-the-legacy-of-howard-thurman-mystic-and-theologian/7895/?xid=PS_smithsonian.

8. Howard Thurman, *With Head and Heart: The Autobiography of Howard Thurman* (Boston: Mariner Books, 1981), 41, 60–61.

9. Howard Thurman, *Mysticism and the Experience of Love* (Wallingford, Pa.: Pendle Hill, 1961).

10. Howard Thurman, "World Tomorrow," December 1928, reprinted in Fluker, *Papers of Howard Washington Thurman*, 1:145–51.

11. Ibid.

12. Dixie and Eisenstadt, *Visions of a Better World*, 73.

13. Howard Thurman, *Footprints of a Dream: The Story of the Church for the Fellowship of All Peoples* (Eugene, Oreg.: Wipf & Stock, 1959), 24.

14. Ibid.

15. Dixie and Eisenstadt, *Visions of a Better World*, 95.

16. Ibid., 108.

17. Ibid., 117.

18. Ibid., 149.

19. Thurman, *Footprints of a Dream*, 31.

20. Thurman, *With Head and Heart*, 98–99.

21. Ibid., 141–42.

22. "Biographical Essay," in *The Papers of Howard Washington Thurman*, vol. 3, *The Bold Adventure, September 1943–May 1949*, ed. Walter Fluker et al. (Columbia: University of South Carolina Press, 2015), xxiii.

23. Thurman to Alfred G. Fisk, 19 May 1944, in Fluker, *Papers of Howard Washington Thurman*, 3:64.

24. Howard Thurman, "Commitment," in Thurman, *For the Inward Journey*, 13.

25. Thurman, *For the Inward Journey*, 13, 21; Thurman, "The Fellowship Church of All Peoples," *Common Ground* 5 (Spring 1945): 29–31; reprinted in Fluker, *Papers of Howard Washington Thurman*, 3:125–27.

26. Thurman, *Footprints of a Dream*, 21; *Meditations of the Heart*, 120–21.

27. Thurman, *Footprints of a Dream*, 44–45, 47.

28. Ibid., 97.

29. Thurman, *For the Inward Journey*, 122.

30. Howard Thurman, *Strange Freedom: The Best of Howard Thurman on Religious Experience and Public Life*, ed. Walter Earl Fluker and Catherine Tumber (Boston: Beacon Press, 1988), 13; Thurman, *With Head and Heart*, 160–61.

31. Thurman, *Footprints of a Dream*, 52.

32. Ibid., 70.

33. See the Howard Thurman Listening Room at http://archives.bu.edu/web/howard-thurman/virtual-listening-room.

34. Lerone Bennett Jr., "Howard Thurman: 20th Century Holy Man," *Ebony*, February 1978, 84; Benita Eisler, "Keeping the Faith," *Nation*, January 5, 1980, 24; Gary Dorrien, "True Religion, Mystical Unity, and the Disinherited: Howard Thurman and the Black Social Gospel," *American Journal of Theology and Philosophy* 39 (January 2018): 74–99, quote on 91.

35. Thurman, *Strange Freedom*, 68.

36. Thurman, *For the Inward Journey*, 215, 223, 225.

37. Thurman, "The Will to Segregation," 1943; reprinted in Thurman, *Strange Freedom*, 211–19 (quote on 219).

38. King's speech of December 4, 1955 is reproduced at http://www.digitalhistory.uh.edu/disp_textbook.cfm?smtid=3&psid=3625.

39. Thurman, *For the Inward Journey*, 122; *Jesus and the Dispossessed*, 29–31.

40. Ibid., 147.

41. Ibid., 159.

42. Ibid., 162.

43. Ibid., 185, 188, 193

44. Ibid., 38, 43.

45. Ibid., 278–79.

46. Ibid., 280.

47. Thurman, *Strange Freedom*, 12.

48. Ibid., 117.

49. Thurman, *Mysticism and the Experience of Love* .

50. Thurman, *Strange Freedom*, 28.

51. Ibid., 33.

52. Dixie and Eisenstadt, *Visions of a Better World*, 181.

53. "Racial Roots and Religion: An Interview with Howard Thurman," *The Christian Century* 90 (May 9, 1973): 533–35.

54. "Introduction," in Thurman, *Strange Freedom*, 13; and Thurman, *With Head and Heart*, 160–61.

CHAPTER 3.
THE BLUES AND GOSPEL TRAIN

1. I have developed this point much further in Paul Harvey, *Christianity and Race in the American South: A History* (Chicago: University of Chicago Press, 2016).

2. Sarah Gardner and Karen Cox, eds., *Reassessing the 1930s South* (Baton Rouge: Louisiana State University Press, 2018).

3. Howard Thurman, *Deep River and the Negro Spiritual Speaks of Life and Death*, reprint ed. (Philadelphia: Friends United Press, 1975).

4. Randall Stephens, "Where Else Did They Copy Their Styles but from Church Groups?": Rock 'n' Roll and Pentecostalism in the 1950s," *Church History* 85 (March 2016): 107. See the fuller version of Stephens's argument in Randall Stephens, *The Devil's Music: How Christians Inspired, Condemned, and Embraced Rock 'N' Roll* (Cambridge, Mass.: Harvard University Press, 2017).

5. Jerma Jackson, *Singing in My Soul: Black Gospel Music in a Secular Age* (Chapel Hill: University of North Carolina Press, 1993).

6. Will Hermes, "Why Sister Rosetta Tharpe Belongs in the Rock and Roll Hall of Fame," *Rolling Stone* online, *https://www.rollingstone.com /music/music-features/why-sister-rosetta-tharpe-belongs-in-the-rock-and-roll -hall-of-fame-123738/.*

7. Gayle Wald, *Shout, Sister, Shout: The Untold Story of Rock-and-Roll Trailblazer Sister Rosetta Tharpe* (Boston: Beacon Press, 2007), 9.

8. Jackson, "Sister Rosetta Tharpe"; *Sister Rosetta Tharpe: Complete Recorded Works in Chronological Order*, vols. 1–3 (Document Records, 1996).

9. Gayle Wald, *Shout, Sister, Shout: The Untold Story of Rock-and-Roll Trailblazer Sister Rosetta Tharpe* (Boston: Beacon Press, 2007). Much of the material on Tharpe throughout this chapter is taken from this outstanding biography by Wald, and the accompanying film, *Sister Rosetta Tharpe: The Godmother of Rock and Roll*, which is available at *https://vimeo.com/101093967*.

10. Listen to the recording at https://www.youtube.com/watch?v=6Xd NA1RCL5M.

11. Wald, *Shout, Sister, Shout*, xi.

12. Ibid., 71–72.

13. Ibid., 156.

14. Ibid., 178, 184.

15. Ibid., 186.

16. Ibid., 216.

17. Robert Hilburn, *Johnny Cash: The Life* (Boston: Back Bay Books, 2013), 70.

18. Hilburn, *Johnny Cash*, 9; Michael Streissguth, *Johnny Cash: The Biography* (Philadelphia: De Capo Press, 2006), 29.

19. Hilburn, *Johnny Cash*, 70; Cash quoted in Stephens, *The Devil's Music*, 38.

20. Hilburn, *Johnny Cash*, 104.

21. Jacob M. Held, "Til Things Get Better: Hope and Redemption in Black," in *Johnny Cash and Philosophy: The Burning Ring of Truth*, ed. John Huss and David Werther (Chicago: Open Court, 2008), 127.

22. Streissguth, *Johnny Cash*, 155.

23. Hilburn, *Johnny Cash*, 375, 446; Paul Harvey, *Moses, Jesus, and the Trickster in the Evangelical South* (Athens: University of Georgia Press, 2011), 129; Stephens, *The Devil's Music*, 60; Streissguth, *Johnny Cash*, 180–81.

24. Hilburn, *Johnny Cash*, 465.

25. Hilburn, *Johnny Cash*, 538.

26. For an astute analysis of the meaning of "hard religion," see John Hayes, *Hard, Hard Religion: Interracial Faith in the Poor South* (Chapel Hill: University of North Carolina Press, 2017). See also George Vecsey, "Cash's 'Gospel Road' Film Is Renaissance for Him," orig. 1973, reprinted in *Ring of Fire: The Johnny Cash Reader*, ed. Michael Streissguth (Cambridge, Mass.: Da Capo Press, 2002), 126; "The Beast in Me," from *American Recordings* (Compact Disc, Lost Highway Records, 1994); Billy Jo Shaver, "Jesus Was Our Savior, Cotton Was Our King," Sony Music Entertainment, 1974; "Personal Jesus" and "Redemption Song" from Johnny Cash, *American IV: The Man Comes*

Around (Compact Disc, Lost Highway, 2002); Ted Olsen, "Johnny Cash's Song of Redemption," *Christianity Today* 47 (November 2003), reprinted in *Ring of Fire: The Johnny Cash Reader*, ed. Michael Streissguth (Cambridge, Mass.: Da Capo Press, 2002), 60–62.

27. Jesse W. Butler, "Cash Value: The Authenticity of Johnny Cash," in *Johnny Cash and Philosophy: The Burning Ring of Truth*, ed. John Huss and David Werther (Chicago: Open Court, 2008), 14–15.

28. Nick Deriso, "The Band, 'The Night They Drove Old Dixie Down' from *The Band* (1969): Across the Great Divide," September 24, 2013, http:// somethingelsereviews.com/2013/09/26/across-the-great-divide-the-band -the-night-they-drove-old-dixie-down-from-the-band-1969/.

29. Shmoop Editorial Team, "The Weight Meaning," *Shmoop University, Inc.*, Last modified November 11, 2008, https://www.shmoop.com/the-band -the-weight/meaning.html.

INDEX

CPSIA information can be obtained
at www.ICGtesting.com
Printed in the USA
LVHW031602300621
691479LV00009B/1073

9 780820 355924